T0209570

GOD
IS ENOUGH
Encouragement for Heavy Hearts

Jean D. McLaurine

WESTBOW
PRESS®
A DIVISION OF THOMAS NELSON
& ZONDERVAN

WestBow Press books may be ordered through booksellers or by contacting:

WestBow Press
A Division of Thomas Nelson & Zondervan
1663 Liberty Drive
Bloomington, IN 47403
www.westbowpress.com
1 (866) 928-1240

ISBN: 978-1-9736-5299-1 (sc)
ISBN: 978-1-9736-5301-1 (hc)
ISBN: 978-1-9736-5300-4 (e)

Library of Congress Control Number: 2019901318

Print information available on the last page.

WestBow Press rev. date: 02/11/2019

CONTENTS

CHAPTER 1

INTRODUCTION

Several years ago, while I was recuperating from lung surgery I had a lot of time to think about what I would do with all my tapes and notes that seemed so valuable to me. I began to write these messages down and it came to me that someone else could benefit from them also. It didn't seem to be a book at first but as it began to grow it turned into a book which is written in loving memory of Mrs. Ollie Hough. I first met her at the home of my dear friend Kathryn Knight in Nashville, TN when she was visiting here from Africa and various other places in the 1970's.

During World War II, this humble servant was not only a great bible teacher but a prayer warrior that spent much time in Knoxville organizing prayer groups. There were so many desperate times during those years and needs that only God could meet. People would go into these meeting places asking for prayer. They spent many hours in prayer and much of the time they would stay all night.

I was really blessed when she would spend time teaching and praying with the group in Nashville. What I would like to do in this book is to show in my small way what she firmly believed to be the trouble in so many lives. Mrs. Hough would say that we do not really know God. We know about Him and we read the scriptures and we think we know Him, but are we really trusting and living in obedience to His will? How much time do we spend praising and thanking Him for all His blessings? We call on the Lord in times of trouble, but we don't always allow Him to direct our lives. To know the Lord is to love Him and put Him in first place. This will transform a life, and it will bring about an intensified awareness of God's presence, an eagerness to hear and read the Word and a dedication to intercessory prayer. God yearns to show us His power in our time just as He did in days of old. I hope these truths will increase every reader's faith in the many promises of God. May it bring joy, peace and encouragement to all heavy hearts.

CHAPTER 2

THE KEY

I n the hand of every redeemed soul, God has placed a key that will unlock the treasury of heaven and bring to our lives the unlimited resources of God. This golden key is prayer. Prayer is the mightiest weapon that God has given to man. In the Word of God, we read that prayer made a way through the Red Sea and brought mighty deliverance for the children of Israel. Prayer closed the mouths of lions, quenched the fury of fire, stopped the sun in its course, held back the rain on the earth for the space of three-and-one-half years, brought the dead back to life, and brought countless other miracles.

In the twelfth chapter of Acts, we read that stone walls, double chains, soldiers, keepers, and iron gates all gave way, and the mighty Roman Empire as represented by Herod was rendered absolutely impotent before the power of prayer — the key that releases the mighty power of God.

Since it is true that God has placed this key in the hands of all believers, why are so many weak and defeated? Why are so many fearful and anxious? Why are their lives so powerless? The answer is three-fold. In the first place, many neglect to use the key.

God says, "You do not have because you do not ask God" (James 4:2). "Ask and it will be given to you" (Matt. 7:7). How sad it is to see God's children weak and defeated, trying to stand in their

3

own strength and to solve their own problems they bear their own burdens even when God has said, "The Lord is at hand. Be anxious for nothing; but in everything by prayer ... let your requests be made known to God" (Phil. 4:5–6 NKJV).

Secondly, some are not benefited by the key because they do not use it in the right way.

> When you ask, you do not receive, because you ask with wrong motives, that you may spend what you get on your pleasures. (James 4:3)

Many prayers are prompted by selfish motives, and therefore do not prevail to open God's storehouse.

In third place, many do not have the faith to wield this weapon of prayer.

> And without faith it is impossible to please God, because anyone who comes to Him must believe that He exists and that He rewards those who earnestly seek Him. (Heb. 11:6)

Faith is the force that turns the key. Lack of faith is due to a need of the Spirit in our lives, for "so then faith comes by hearing, and hearing by the Word of God" (Rom. 10:17 NKJV). Faith is produced by the Holy Spirit in an obedient heart.

> Dear friends, if our hearts do not condemn us, we have confidence before God and receive from him anything we ask because we obey His commands and do what pleases him. (1 John 3:21-22)

From these and many other passages of Scripture, we see that it is the one who is living on a high spiritual plane who has power in prayer.

Our greatest need today is the kind of praying that Daniel did to shake the Babylonian empire. We need persistent prayer like the widow where the judge had to arise from the bench, postpone business, and attend to her urgent needs. This is the kind of prayer that is born in the very heart of God's Word, and it is the only weapon we can use today to touch the invisible foe! We may never know until we reach eternity what we have been spared through the ministry of intercession.

Remember the prayer that Elijah the prophet prayed at Mt. Carmel.

> Answer me, O Lord, answer me, so these people
> will know that you, O Lord, are God, and that you
> are turning their hearts back again. (1 Kings 18:37)

We may need to call down showers of blessings upon God's people who are in such dry and barren situations. Believe that God's will is being done according to the greatness of His power and wisdom. Don't under estimate God's ability to make a way for you when one doesn't seem possible, but believe like Abraham.

> Yet he did not waver through unbelief regarding
> the promise of God, but was strengthened in his
> faith and gave glory to God, being fully persuaded
> that God had power to do what he had promised.
> (Rom 4:20–21)

May God help us to yield to Him and be so filled with His Holy Spirit that we can pray with a faith that will be an irresistible force.

CHAPTER 3

BROKEN FOR CHRIST

I t was a great discovery when I realized that God tells us He uses despised, weak, and broken things. We place such high values upon natural ability, talents, gifts, and special training. But God says He is looking for those who in their weakness and brokenness know that by themselves they can do nothing. In I Corinthians He says,

> Not many of you were wise by human standards, not many were influential, not many were of noble birth. But God chose the foolish things of the world to shame the wise; God chose the weak things of the world to shame the strong. He chose the lowly things of this world and the despised things that are not to nullify the things that are, so that no one may boast before Him. (1 Cor. 1:26–29)

We are told from the time we are little children that broken toys are to be thrown away, broken dishes and glass are to be discarded, and broken furniture goes to the junk pile. We assume that people who have had failures, broken relationships, disappointments, broken homes, broken dreams, and even broken bodies are of no great value in this world and especially to a holy God. When you are lonely and broken in spirit, it's easy to feel like a total failure. Yet our great heavenly Father uses these very things to draw us close to Him.

Are you being broken today? Beloved, the Lord will take all the broken pieces and make them fit into His plan and purpose for your life. When He finishes, it will be filled with wisdom and beauty. He just wants us to hand it all over to Him who delights in making all things new! The things that we look at now as trials and tragedies may be viewed at a later date differently. We read in Isaiah 48:10, "See, I have refined you, though not as silver; I have tested you in the furnace of affliction. For My own sake, I do this."

If we never had a problem or a need, in all likelihood, we would become all puffed up and very proud. It seems that sometimes it takes years of heartaches before our spiritual eyes are opened to the truth. As we study the lives of the saints, we can see how the Lord had to allow them to be broken to little pieces before He could greatly use them. Over and over in the scriptures we can see how God uses the broken things to gain the victory. In the book of Psalms, we see how David suffered with a broken and contrite heart after he sinned. In the book of Judges, we see how God used Gideon and the three hundred men to overcome the enemy with only trumpets, pitchers, and lamps. The lamps were put inside the pitchers, so they could not be seen until they were broken. As they went into battle, they didn't even carry swords. Each man carried a trumpet in one hand and a pitcher in the other. Gideon posted his three hundred men in three groups around the Midianites' camp. At a certain time that night they blew their trumpets and broke the pitchers so that the light shined out. The enemy awoke and started thrashing around with their swords at each other. The Midianites soon fled over the hills into the tall timber and out of that area. This gave Gideon and the Israelites a tremendous victory!

From the viewpoint of human wisdom, God used utterly foolish and inadequate means to bring down the walls of Jericho. There was the blast on the ram's horn, the sound of the trumpets, and the shouting of the people. Can you imagine how foolish this must have sounded to the people? Joshua had been trained well in the wilderness and had seen many miracles. He knew and believed that God meant what He said. When they had marched around the city the seventh time, the priests blew the trumpets, the people shouted with a great shout, and the wall came tumbling down. The people went rushing into the city to take it. They didn't have to fight at all, for the city was taken by faith.

Hebrews 11 tells us how faith like Joshua worked in the lives of God's choicest servants as they met the world head on and overcame by faith. Joseph is another example given.

Joseph was sold into slavery by his jealous brothers, and he suffered unjustly for years as his hopes and dreams were dashed. When he was a young man, God gave to him a dream that he would in some way rule over his brothers. He went into Egypt and was thrown into prison from a false accusation by the wife of Pharaoh's official. It must have been a very dark time for Joseph, but there is nothing to indicate that he was waiting impatiently or writing letters proclaiming his innocence. It is never written that he had a complaining spirit. He was learning to trust his father's God. Jacob's heart was broken for he thought his son was dead. Joseph was thirty years old before he went into service for Pharaoh as his second-in-command. His dream finally came true! Because of all the suffering, God was able to use him mightily to feed his people through the famine years that came. Jacob and his family could not have survived had they stayed in the land of Palestine. Joseph brought them into the land of Goshen, which was the best part of Egypt. It is in that land that God made them a nation, sheltered from the rest of the world. Joseph never became bitter toward his brothers, but he became a bigger man. He realized that God had sent him there before them so that he might be used to help preserve lives. God had great plans for Israel.

We are not victims of chance; we can see this as we study the life of Joseph. If God knows what is best for me, then how can I possibly take my life out of His capable hands? Our earthly fathers make promises, and they are often broken. However, we are to look to our heavenly Father for His Word stands true forever.

You will recall the day Jesus was in Capernaum teaching and four men brought a friend to Him to be healed. They couldn't get to him, so they took the man on the roof of the house and let him down with a mat through the tiles into the middle of the crowd right in front of Jesus. That had to have caused quite a commotion. Can you imagine what a shock that must have been when this big hole in the roof opens up and a man on a mat comes down at you? There must have been debris flying everywhere. But Jesus looked at the man and said, "Take heart, son; your sins are forgiven" (Matt. 9:2). What faith those four friends had! Do we love our friends enough to break up a roof or turn things upside down to bring them to Jesus? Would we make the effort to bring broken bodies to the Lord? The four friends knew that Jesus had the power to set men free and to heal any kind of brokenness. They showed their true faith in the Lord and expressed a genuine love for their friend. So much of what we do is not done in love. When we become more like God, who loves the just and the unjust, we will be able to love one another. A church is known by the quality of ambassadors it is sending out into the world. When we begin to show an honest compassion for people, and genuine love for one another, the power and presence of God in our lives will flow out to bring broken men and women into the kingdom.

CHAPTER 4

HUMILITY AND FAITH

M oses was learned in all the wisdom of the Egyptians and was mighty in word and in deeds. He was allowed to make his first attempt to deliver his people in the energy of the flesh and failed badly. He was rejected by his brethren and was so gripped by powerlessness and hopelessness that he fled from Egypt, and lived in exile for forty years. He supposed that his brethren would know that God by His hand would deliver them, but he failed because he trusted in his natural ability. He was reduced to extreme helplessness and utter nothingness before God could send him back to Egypt to deliver them. He had to suffer forty hidden years in the desert before he learned that it is not by might nor by power, but by the Lord. He learned faith in God and the obedience of faith by humiliation and suffering.

He was sure of being in God's plan when he went back to deliver his people. God said in Acts 7:34, "I have indeed seen the oppression of my people in Egypt. I... have come down to set them free. Now come, I will send you back to Egypt." Moses was surrendered to God and yielded to His purpose. We know that by his chosen name "The servant of the Lord". He knew the promises and so completely trusted in God's faithfulness that at God's bidding, he launched himself and three million people absolutely on His care with the assurance that His faithfulness could not fail.

How great was the faith of Moses! When he had grown to maturity and became great, he refused to be called the son of Pharaoh's daughter, because he preferred rather to suffer the hardships and bear the shame of the people of God, rather than to have the fleeting enjoyment of a sinful life. He considered the shame borne for Christ to be greater riches than all the wealth of Egypt, for he looked forward and away to the reward. By faith, he left Egypt behind him, but held staunchly to his purpose, and endured steadfastly as one that gazed on Him who is invisible. What he saw by faith, the spiritual wealth and reward was so much better than the wealth of Egypt that he cheerfully took the path of affliction, self-denial and reproach that led to them.

The writer of Hebrews gives us the secret of the marvels wrought by the heroes of faith. We make a great mistake in attributing to these men extra-ordinary qualities of courage and strength of body and soul. They were no different from other men, except for their faith.

They had a marvelous faculty of faith which is the capacity of the human heart for God. Four times in the eleventh chapter of Hebrews this is cited as the secret of all Moses did for his people. All the blessings that God bestowed on Israel, that rebellious and stiff-necked people, came through the channel of Moses's faith. It was through Moses's faith that God fulfilled His promise to Abraham, Isaac, and Jacob.

Faith comes by hearing and hearing by the Word of God! God has so much He wants to give us. His desire is to open the windows of heaven and pour out a blessing, that there shall not be room enough to receive it! Dear saints, we are to humble ourselves before the Lord and live by faith, not by what we see, and if we are to be faithful to God, we cannot sit around in discouragement and doubt. Let us then encourage each other in the faith, and put away all unbelief. The Lord is full of compassion and invites us to come at any time of the day or night, so we may boldly say, "The Lord is my helper; I will not be afraid. What can man do to me" (Heb. 13:6). He is with you no matter what lies the enemy may whisper.

Faith believes God and His Word even when circumstances, emotions, and all human reason urges against it. Moses had that kind of faith. He knew God would not let him down, and he was very aware of God's presence. The people were always complaining and couldn't seem to remember how God had delivered them from the hand of the enemy, watched over them, provided food and water, and clothes that didn't wear out. It is faith in His promises that stills the storms of fear, worry and anxiety in the heart. That is why we should never neglect the study of His Word. There is no explaining the inner peace and strength that He will give in times of need. His grace is sufficient indeed! I pray that as we grow in the grace and knowledge of the Lord that we will be able to believe and trust Him more and more. May we be able to say to Him, "The Lord is the strength of my life" (Ps. 27:16 NKJV). Be strong and take heart, all you who hope in the Lord.

There are many Christians who are good for the short sprint but quickly fade. Faithfulness requires that we press on when we are exhausted, when we are discouraged, when we are fearful, and when we think our lives are coming unglued. We must learn to take God at His Word and to move on in faith. He will see us through!

CHAPTER 5

DELIVERANCE

Have you been brought to the Red Sea experience? We read in Exodus 14 that the children of Israel were being led out of Egypt by Moses. When they learned that Pharaoh and his army were fast approaching them, they were terrified. It was a fearsome place to be in.

They were at the very bank of the Red Sea with no way to get through it, and Pharaoh's mighty army was right behind them. Have you ever been in a tight corner like that when all human strength and resources had been exhausted, and seemingly there was no way out? I know I have many times. They couldn't turn back without the army capturing them and taking them back into slavery again. There was no way to turn to the left or right, and all they could see in front was a vast sea to drown in. What an impossible situation to be in! Now what is God going to do?

By shutting His people in on every side so that there was no way out, they had to look up to Him. There was no escape unless God intervened. He had told Moses that He would be with them and deliver all the people, but in that hour of great need they began to panic. When they were in the land of Egypt, they cried out to God for deliverance. He made the way for them to leave, but the minute they were in danger, they wanted to return.

These poor defenseless people were caught between the devil and the deep blue sea! They knew they were going to be slaughtered by the powerful Egyptian army. Unless God moved on their behalf, they were doomed. So many times the Lord allows a crisis situation that He might show His power of deliverance. Moses told the people "Do not be afraid. Stand firm and you will see the deliverance the Lord will bring you today. The Egyptians you see today you will never see again. The Lord will fight for you; you need only be still" (Exod. 14:13–14). As they stepped out in faith, the water before them turned into dry ground. The waters parted and made a wall on each side until they crossed. As the Egyptians pursued them, the waters returned and the Lord over threw the enemy in the midst of the sea. As the Israelites saw what the Lord did to Pharaoh and his army, they feared the Lord and believed Him and His servant Moses!

God has shut many of His children in on every side, and humanly speaking there is no way out of the complex problems that we face today. When giants are facing you on every corner, it is surely tempting to think that God has forgotten His promises to help. Discouragement comes in like a flood and overwhelms you. Our trials and afflictions may be great, many and varied, but dear saints, may we get our eyes off of our enemies, the problems themselves, and the things that cause us to lose hope. We need the mighty tide of God to roll out His power upon us that our faith might grow stronger in these difficult times. Let us keep looking to our great God who says that nothing is too hard for Him. Our Deliverer delights in meeting the needs of His children. He is still the same God today as He was with Moses and the children of Israel. What He did for them was a miracle. They didn't even get their feet wet. They saw God's great power when He delivered them out of Egypt, and they saw it again when He took them across the Red Sea on dry ground.

Upon reaching the other side of the Red Sea they were jubilant, and no longer were they complaining to Moses. In the book of Exodus we are told that they sang a song of praise to the Lord.

I will sing to the Lord, for He is highly exalted. The horse and its rider He has hurled into the sea. The Lord is my strength and my song; He has become my salvation. He is my God, and I will praise Him, my father's God, and I will exalt Him. (Exod. 15:1–2)

The song is truly a beautiful praise to the Lord for working such a miracle for them.

The Lord delivered David many times, and the Psalms are full of his cries for help. He knew that God had a way to get him out when he was in a difficult spot. In Psalm 50:15 we read, "call upon me in the day of trouble; I will deliver you, and you will honor me." In Psalm 55 David called,

> I call to God, and the Lord saves me. Evening, morning and noon I call out in distress, and He hears my voice. He ransoms me unharmed from the battle waged against me, even though many oppose me. (Ps. 55:16–18)

Whatever drives you to your knees, don't despise it. It was in these disastrous times that God was able to show David many things in his life. He was humbled. Life became so very precious.

God is teaching and training us while we are here on this earth that we might grow in Him. There are many of God's children who walk with Him for a short while but become faint-hearted and soon fade away. Faithfulness requires that we press on in His strength. Let us learn to triumph in tough times. As long as God is with us, there is nothing that is impossible. If you are really trusting God, He is going to see to it that every force that is against you will be destroyed.

We are so like the children of Israel wandering in the wilderness. When we can feel His presence or see Him working, it is easy to trust; however, when we face such dark circumstances and feel trapped within them, the doubting begins. Conditions often seem to make it impossible for God to meet our needs. In our heart we limit

Him because we do not trust His faithfulness and goodness. What a difference it makes as we get into the study of His Word and claim the promises for that particular burden. Our Lord has said that He would never leave us or forsake us. So fear not, dear saint, for the deeper the darkness of despair, the greater need of appealing to the one and only deliverer. He has never failed us. Deliverance is sure! God Himself will put a new song into your heart. When you get to that place of refuge, your life will never be the same. Praise the Lord!

CHAPTER 6

BELIEVING GOD

There were twelve men of Israel that Moses sent to spy out the Promised Land. Ten saw the giants and were frightened. They came back filled with unbelief that God could be with them and conquer those walled cities. The other two men were Joshua and Caleb who believed that God would give them the victory.

God was a reality to them, for they had not forgotten how He had brought about the miracle of the Red Sea. Caleb stood up before the people and said, "We should go up and take possession of the land, for we can certainly do it" (Num. 13:30). But the people were filled with unbelief and just couldn't trust God to fight for them. What a tremendous influence for evil the ten faint-hearted men were! The entire congregation of Israel was gripped by their fearful, unbelieving spirit.

If you are facing a seemingly impossible situation, I hope this teaching helps you look to God for your answer. Maybe you are dealing with a broken relationship with a family member, overwhelming financial burdens, the frustration of ill health or you know someone who is. In any of these cases, God does not leave us without His help. In 2 Chronicles 13, we find an Old Testament event that gives some understanding of how we can call on God's wonderful power through faithful, confident prayer and trust Him to give us the victory. It looked like the troops of Judah were going to be defeated, but God's people cried to the Lord and He defeated the enemy. This victory overcame impossible odds because they trusted in the Lord.

Whatever you face, and whatever task you have before you, you can be confident that God will give you the resources and inner strength to complete it. Satan will do everything he can to oppose you, but "greater is He who is in you, than he who is in the world" (1 John 4:4). We can surely claim this testimony today with other believers "I would have lost heart, unless I had believed That I would see the goodness of the Lord In the land of the living" (Ps. 27:16 NKJV). God cannot use fearful and faint-hearted soldiers in His army.

Only Joshua and Caleb were allowed to go into the Promised Land forty years later. The judgment of God was upon them, and they wandered in the dessert until all that generation died. They had turned from the land, but they were actually more afraid of the wilderness than of going into the walled cities with the giants. Their children along with Caleb and Joshua were brought safely into the land forty years later.

This journey of life is full of difficult decisions, and sometimes we really don't know what direction we should take. For the children of Israel, it was plain and simple that they didn't have the faith to believe God. The only other choice was to go into the wilderness. They made the wrong decision. Have you ever made the wrong decision? We all have at times made tragic mistakes when we insisted on doing things without God's help. Sometimes we make a decision and then ask God to bless it. We also have to suffer the consequences of these mistakes. Sometimes it takes a lot of courage to step out in faith, but the Lord has promised to deliver the needy who cry out, the afflicted who have no one to help. We all have mountains in our lives, and there are people or things that threaten our progress in this walk with God.

God always has a way of making obstacles serve His purpose,

and this is a lesson for Christians involved in a spiritual battle, no matter what the odds, no matter what the enemy may be. If we commit our cause to Jesus and depend on Him, He will give us the victory!

The Canaanite woman had the faith to believe that Jesus would heal her demon possessed daughter. He said to her, "Woman, you have great faith! Your request is granted". Her daughter was healed from that very hour. By faith, Abraham, when called to go to a place he would later receive as his inheritance, obeyed and went, even though he did not know where he was going. By faith, Abraham, even though he was past age and Sarah herself was barren was enabled to become a father because he considered Him faithful who had made the promise.

Abraham believed God even though he was one hundred years old. Joshua believed God and the walls of Jericho fell after the people had marched around them for seven days. Daniel trusted in God, and he came out of the lion's den unscathed. Faith that shuts the mouths of lions has to be more than a pious hope that they won't bite! Noah believed God and built an ark even though it had never rained on the earth. Job believed God and said, "Though He slay me, yet will I trust Him" (Job 13:15 NKJV).

We saints serve that same God. He has been looking for men and women who will trust Him to do the impossible. A father brought his boy who had a dumb and deaf spirit one day to the disciples of Jesus. It proved to be an impossible case for them to deal with. When Jesus arrived at the scene, He said to the father, "If you can believe, all things are possible to him who believes" (Mark 9:23 NKJV). Let us learn to bring our hard cases to Jesus and really trust Him to do what lies beyond human power and wisdom. We have a God who delights in impossibilities. If you believe this to be true, nothing will lie beyond the reach of your prayer except what lies outside God's will for you.

CHAPTER 7

CLAIM YOUR INHERITANCE

As we look into the book of Joshua, we learn that the children of Israel were told by God to go into Jericho and conquer it. God had said to Joshua,

> Be strong and courageous because you will lead these people to inherit the land I swore to their forefathers to give them. Be strong and very courageous ... Do not be terrified, do not be discouraged for the Lord your God will be with you wherever you go. (Josh. 1:6–9)

Joshua was one of the twelve men who went to spy in the land of Canaan, and only he and Caleb came back with a good report. Because the others were afraid and did not believe God, they had to wander in the wilderness for forty years until all of them had died.

Only their children with Joshua and Caleb were allowed to go in and take possession of the land. Even though God had told them the land was theirs they had to go in and claim it! God said to the

Israelites, "I will give you every place where you set your foot, as I promised Moses" (Jos 1:3). The people realized that crossing the Jordon River into the land of Canaan was a great event for they would be facing their enemies. The entire nation took this step of faith together. As the feet of the priests touched the water, it was as though a great dam had been made, for they walked across the Jordan River on dry ground. God had performed another miracle for them for the waters were at flood stage! They were then instructed to take twelve stones out of the Jordon, which represented the twelve tribes of Israel, and they were put on the west bank as a reminder to their children of God's great power at work for them. Every victory that Israel won was given by God. Joshua was a very capable leader for he had served with Moses on that long journey in the wilderness. He was courageous but totally dependent upon his God. Though he must have thought God's methods were strange in conquering the walled city of Jericho, he also trusted and followed His instructions.

Just as Israel faced giants in the land, we face our own giants. However, we do not wrestle with flesh and blood but with spiritual enemies. We have no human weapons with which to conquer these giants, but must look to the Lord and be fully equipped with the armor of God. He has told us to claim the victory that Christ won on Calvary's cross over all the work of the enemy in our lives. God was a reality to Joshua, and he was not afraid to shout and proclaim the victory even before it was an actual fact. Dear saint, reach out that hand of faith and take that which God has promised you. Pray that God will give you the faith that moves mountains. Don't be afraid but be very courageous as you face difficult situations.

Caleb is a wonderful example of a man who was brave enough to claim his inheritance. He said,

> I however, followed the Lord my God wholeheartedly ... So here I am today, eighty-five years old! I am still strong today as when Moses sent me out; I'm just as vigorous to go out to battle now

CHAPTER 8

TAKE A STAND

God made no mistake in choosing Joshua to lead the nation of Israel. He had served Moses on their journey in the wilderness, so he had a wonderful role model. He was encouraged and instructed along the way, and he had seen how God had provided and protected as they wandered for forty years. God said to Joshua, "Be strong and courageous ... for the Lord your God will be with you wherever you go" (Josh. 1:9). Joshua was just an average man who had a heart that was sold out to God, and this is what the Lord is looking for today. He was mightily used to deliver the nation of Israel from their enemies. Joshua called all the people together and said,

> Throw away the gods your forefathers worshiped beyond the River and in Egypt, and serve the Lord. But if serving the Lord seems undesirable to you, then choose for yourselves this day whom you will serve, whether the gods your forefathers served beyond the River, or the gods of the Amorites, in whose land you are living. But as for me and my household, we will serve the Lord. (Josh. 24:14–15)

This was a tremendous challenge to the nation of Israel, and it should be for us today as we look back and see the results of sinful disobedience. Why aren't we as believers taking a stand for God today? We need men of stature like Joshua that will not be afraid to call their families back to the Lord.

Israel had seen God perform miracle after miracle for them, but after they entered the land they were so engulfed with prosperity and pleasure that they began to drift away from Him. They would stay close and serve Him for a while after a great victory. They had such short memories they would soon forget what He had done. Joshua gave the people a review of their history as a nation and God's gracious dealings with them through the years. The Israelites answered his challenge:

> Far be it from us to forsake the Lord to serve other gods! It was the Lord our God Himself who brought us and our forefathers up out of Egypt, from that land of slavery, and performed those great signs before our eyes. He protected us on our entire journey and among all the nations through which we traveled. ... We too will serve the Lord, because He is our God. (Josh. 24:16–18)

It is easy for us to look back and wonder how they could have fallen away so quickly, but what about our nation? What about us? We have been so blessed in this country. God has allowed us to prosper more than any other nation, yet we are following other gods just as Israel did. The same old story repeated itself. The nation of Israel did serve the Lord for a while. Then they turned away, did evil and forsook God, followed their own pleasure and judgment came. They would cry out to God to deliver them. They would repent and serve Him for a while. Then they would fall back again.

Isaiah gives three steps that cause the downfall of nations: (1) spiritual apostasy; (2) moral awfulness; and (3) political anarchy which are the final stage of any nation. These steps have destroyed nations throughout history. There were whole generations in Israel's history who never heard God's Word. In Leviticus 26:18–21, we read that God spoke to the people and said,

> If after all this you will not listen to me, I will punish you for your sins seven times over. I will break down your stubborn pride and make the sky above you like iron and ground beneath you like bronze. Your strength will be spent in vain, because your soil will not yield its crops, nor will the trees of the land yield their fruit. If you remain hostile toward me and refuse to listen to me, I will multiply your afflictions seven times over, as your sins deserve. (Lev. 26:18–21)

God abhors sin, and He will not tolerate it in your life or mine. We are reminded in Proverbs that, "Righteousness exalts a nation, but sin is a disgrace to any people" (Prov. 14:34).

Our children need role models today as never before. It is absolutely necessary that they see men taking places of spiritual leadership in the homes and churches today. Where there are no men, the women have to do it. God will bless in that situation, but when there are no men in the home there must be those in the church that will be role models for our children if we are to serve God in the future. In the book of Deuteronomy, God commanded the people to teach their children that the Word might be passed on from generation to generation. He is seeking godly men and women who will share how God has worked in their lives. The Lord wants to pour out His healing ointment on our families and make them wholesome, powerful and obedient servants of the Lord. Joshua took the spiritual responsibility for his family. He felt more responsible for them than for the nation he led.

Pray for your families. God has given us precious promises for them. Joshua made the decision to serve the Lord regardless of what the others thought. What would happen in America if the world around us could see God at work healing the broken homes?

How far we have gotten away from God today! We have left Him out of our schools, our government, our homes, and even some churches are denying the power of God. Beloved, we don't need better methods or ways. God says, return to me. When we do this, God's presence and power will begin to fill His people again. It is imperative that we hear and obey God's call today for godly men and women to take a stand. He promises to bless the house of the righteous!

Just as Joshua was encouraged and strengthened, we should be encouraging our families. This kind of atmosphere must be created for them. Joshua was always remembering what God had done for them in the past, and he trusted Him fully to be faithful in the future. As he spoke to the people he said, "You know with all your heart and soul that not one of all the good promises the Lord your God gave you has failed. Every promise has been fulfilled, not one has failed" (Josh. 23:14). Trust God, believe His Word about Himself and see His joy pour forth from your life.

CHAPTER 9

CHARACTER

Did you know that the pressures of life reveal where we are with the Lord? We should be reflecting the Lord Jesus Christ, but when the pressures come at us on every side, what the world gets to see is the kind of person we really are on the inside. How do you react in an emergency? It is strange how sweet and nice a person may be at a church meeting, and then completely change into a rude and impolite person at home. "Out of the overflow of the heart the mouth speaks" (Matt. 12:34). True character is flowing through our mouths. We are a witness wherever we go, for people are watching and waiting to see if we are real. There can be mechanical Christians, and there are the genuine Christians. On the battleground we begin to see what we really are. Pressure does very strange things to people! What happens when you're in a hurry and have to wait in a long line at the bank or the grocery, or someone spills a glass of tea on your best tablecloth?

As we look at the life of Saul, we can see how this man who had such a promising future failed miserably because of his pride and folly. He lived a very tragic life, but it didn't start that way. Israel demanded a king from Samuel so that they would be like all the other nations around them. Even when Samuel told them what a king would do to them, they still insisted on having their way.

God gave them Saul, who was a good-looking man that stood a head taller than the others. He was very popular with the people at first, but it didn't take them long to realize what they had done. God had wanted to be their king and direct their lives, as He wants to do for us, but they refused to be different from the nations around them.

As we read in I Samuel, we see how they had to suffer the consequences of their bad national choice! Saul was a man of very weak character. He failed to realize how important character is, and especially in a leader. You have to wonder how he got so far away from his beginnings. He had so much going for him! Saul disobeyed God in the small areas of his life, which shows he didn't take sin seriously. It only led to bigger problems. He didn't understand that spiritual decline is gradual. God removed His spirit from Saul because he had a divided heart. He served God for what he could get out of Him. When he was doing what God wanted him to do, he thought he could obey and profit for himself. At the end of his life the thing he believed in the most was his spear. He disregarded God's prophet and took it upon himself to be priest and prophet.

Saul had learned to be insensitive to spiritual things. When he disobeyed God he used religious reasons for doing it. He went to an all-time low when he consulted with a witch and medium. He totally destroyed everything that was worthwhile in his life. The record seems to indicate that he may have had to watch his own sons die. He had lost his family. The message of his life is for our good. He started out with so much promise, but made several bad decisions and ended up dying in a tragic way. Saul's life was a miserable failure and ended in defeat.

Jesus' character should be woven into the very fabric of our own personality. Our lives should truly count for Him. The only way we will reflect His life is by trusting and obeying Him, and the only way we can do this is to anchor ourselves into God's Word. Proverbs is full of wisdom and knowledge. We are told,

A wise woman builds her house, but with her own hands the foolish one tears hers down. (Prov. 14:1)

Every prudent man acts out of knowledge, but a fool exposes his folly. (Prov. 13:6)

A wife of noble character is her husband's crown, but a disgraceful wife is like decay in his bones. (Prov. 12:4)

A word aptly spoken is like apples of gold in settings of silver. Like an earring of gold or an ornament of fine gold is a wise man's rebuke to a listening ear. Like the coolness of snow at harvest time is a trustworthy messenger to those who send him; he refreshes the spirit of his masters. (Prov. 25:11–13)

There is a story in I Samuel 25 about a beautiful and intelligent woman named of Abigail. Although she was married to a very rich and evil man, Abigail was a woman of noble character. Nabal was a fool who had neither honor nor honesty, but her experience with this man had made her a better woman not a bitter one. David and his army had been protecting Nabal's property for some time. They could have taken some of the cattle for food when they needed it, but they sent word to him asking for it. When he refused, Abigail knew what David would do to him, so she put together a great deal of food and went out to meet him. David's intention was to kill every man that belonged to Nabal. When Abigail saw David she fell at his feet and told him to put the blame on her, and let her gifts be given to his men, and forgive her husband. You are going to be king, so don't do anything you will later regret. This was good advice and David realized it to be. He was very thankful to this woman of noble character that had kept him from an act that would have caused him much grief. Nabal had a big party that night and was very drunk. When he sobered up the next day his wife told him all that had happened. We are told that his heart died within him, and he became as a stone. He died ten days later.

It is always better to put things into God's hands and let Him be the avenger as David did with Nabal. Not every battle is worth winning. Sometimes deeds come back to haunt us when we react in the wrong way. It is difficult, but some things are better off endured. Have you ever done anything that you regret? I have many times. The bag of yesterday's failures is so heavy it disrupts our peace. What can we do? Drag them to Jesus, for He is the only one that can forgive sin and give you peace.

> Therefore, as God's chosen people, holy and dearly loved, clothe yourselves with compassion, kindness, humility, gentleness and patience. Bear with each other and forgive whatever grievances you may have against one another. Forgive as the Lord forgave you. And over all these virtues put on love, which binds them all together in perfect unity. (Col. 3:12–14)

CHAPTER 10

COURAGE AND CONFIDENCE

When God chose David to be king over Israel, He looked beyond his youth and good looks. He could see the inner heart of this young man. God in His foreknowledge knew that David would sin and have many failures; still He knew David's heart. He had a great plan and purpose for this shepherd boy. David loved and trusted God, and underneath was a faith that never faltered. He suffered greatly for the sins he committed, for the Lord chastened him more each time. He could have gone into deep depression over some of the things in his life, but as he came back to God in repentance, we can see the whole book of Psalms is full of prayer, worship and praise. He tells us, "Evening and morning and at noon will I pray, and cry aloud" (Ps. 55:17 NKJV)

Regardless of what our past has been God wants us to call unto Him. He wants to do a new thing in us. It is encouraging to me to see that if He can take men like Jacob and Jonah and use them, He will certainly do the same for you and me. God used the prostitute Rahab because she had the faith and courage to hide the spies when they came to Jericho. In Hebrews 11 there were many others mentioned who through faith conquered kingdoms, administered justice, and gained what was promised; who shut the mouths of lions, quenched the fury of the flames, and escaped the edge of the sword; whose weakness was turned to strength; and who became powerful in battle and routed foreign armies. Others were tortured and persecuted, chained and thrown into prison. All of these were commended for their faith. They truly believed God and had the courage to take their stand throughout all the torture and conflict.

The episode of David and Goliath is one of the most familiar in the Bible. It reveals more than human bravery about David. Even as a boy, he had a heart for God. He didn't volunteer to fight the giant because his people were being shamed, but because Goliath was defying the armies of the living God! As he faced his foe, he testified to his faith in God:

> You come against me with sword and spear, and javelin, but I come against you in the name of the Lord Almighty, the God of the armies of Israel, whom you have defied. This day the Lord will hand you over to me, and I'll strike you down and cut off your head, Today I will give the carcasses of the Philistine army to the birds of the air and the beasts of the earth, and the whole world will know that there is a God in Israel. All those gathered here will know that it is not by sword or spear that the Lord saves, for the battle is the Lord's and He will give all of you into our hands (1 Sam. 17:45–47).

As the giant moved closer to attack him, David ran quickly toward the battle line to meet him. Reaching into his bag and taking out a stone, he slung it and struck the Philistine on the forehead. The stone sank into his forehead, and he fell face down on the ground. David triumphed over the Philistine with a sling and a stone without a sword in his hand. He struck down the Philistine and killed him.

The battle was the Lord's, and the giant was delivered into David's hands just as he had said.

David the king never forgot David the shepherd boy. As we study Psalm twenty-three, we see that it is written by a mature man. He could look back over his life and see all the ups and downs, and this is probably when he could say, the Lord is MY shepherd. David had been tested and tried. He knew all about sheep. They need to be led because they are stubborn and hardheaded animals. He was the same way, ruddy and a very strong-willed man. People that know sheep say that they will not lie down if they are hungry. When we read sheep are lying down in green pastures, it means they have eaten and are ready to rest. We too are like sheep. The Lord promises that if we make Him our shepherd that we can say, I shall not want. He will meet our need for safety, protection, rest and assurance for our tomorrows. He will give us courage and confidence to do His will. He will bring us all the way from green pastures and still waters to the Father's house. The shepherd gave His life for the sheep, and we can now say that He is MY savior and the Lord of MY life!"

David was a man of God who had learned what to do in a crisis. Time after time he ran to his secret place to empty all his fears before the Lord. "In my distress I called upon the Lord, and cried to my God" (2 Sam. 22:7 NKJV). David knew what to do when he became depressed. He began to praise the Lord and to think on God's blessings.

Our hearts sink when we read that a child dies from street violence, or another family is torn apart through divorce or separation. We hear about terrorism at home and abroad, in the air and on the ground. The news gets so discouraging that it is a great relief to turn again to the Bible and read about God's promises to keep us, to give us a future and a hope.

When troubles surround you, you may be tempted to ask, "Does God care for me?" The Psalmist voiced the sentiments of many when he said: "I have no refuge; no one cares for my life" (Ps. 142:4).

How many faithful, loving mothers, overwhelmed by their

burdens at home and other places, have cried anxiously, "Lord, do you not care?" How many godly men worried by pressures in their work or private lives, have whispered, "Lord, do you not care?" That question is answered in those reassuring words of Peter: "He cares for you." You can be positively assured that God does care for you, and if God cares for you and has promised to carry your burdens and concerns. Then nothing should distress you. God's eye is still on you. You have not been forsaken. This word is for you; right from the heart of your caring, loving heavenly father! "The eyes of the Lord are on the righteous, and his ears are attentive to their cry" (Ps. 34:15). Keep crying out to Him. God is teaching you to wholly depend on Him in spite of your circumstances and He also said, "I will never leave you nor forsake you" (Josh. 1:5). Dear saint, what a comfort are those words!

CHAPTER 11

HIDDEN IN HIM

D o you need a place in which you can hide from the pressures of this life; a place that is filled with comfort and peace? Our home should be such a place, but so often it is turmoil. Our body needs a place of rest but it is even more important that our mind is at peace. We spend much of our life fearing evil, and our imagination is absolutely overworked supposing this should happen or what if that should come upon us. Over and over again we read in God's Word that we should fear not or do not worry. We are told, "Do let not your hearts be troubled and do not be afraid" (John 14:27). Why is it that we continue to live in fear when He promises us rest and freedom from this terrible anxiety?

In Colossians, we read that the Lord has provided us a solution to the great problems that face all human beings. He has said, "Set your minds on things above, not on earthly things. For you died, and your life is now hidden with Christ in God" (Col. 3:2). Now we who are God's children are hidden in Him and nothing can touch us unless He permits it.

In the 91st Psalm God tells us that He has prepared for us a refuge, a fortress, and the description is so comforting, such a restful place. "He who dwells in the shelter of the Most High will rest in the shadow of the Almighty. I will say of the Lord, He is my refuge and my fortress, my God in whom I trust ... He will cover you with his feathers, and under his wings you will find refuge; his faithfulness will be your shield and rampart" Ps. 91:1–2,4). God's fortress is so different from the ones we might be familiar with. How would I get into such a place? Beloved, this is a life of faith. We must do as Christ has said, "Abide in Me" (John 15:4). He wants us to come to Him and cast all our burdens upon him and leave them there. Our trouble is that we cast them and then go back and pick them up again. How it must grieve the heart of God when we do not trust Him enough to take care of us, our problems, and our loved ones.

Jesus plainly tells us in Matthew 6,

> Do not worry about your life, what you will eat or drink or about your body, what you will wear. Is not life more important than food, and the body more important than clothes? Look at the birds of the air, they do not sow or reap or store in barns, and yet your heavenly Father feeds them. Are you not more valuable than they? Who of you by worrying can add a single hour to his life? (Matt. 6:25–27)

If we are rejoicing in things, possessions or people, we can never be free from anxiety. Possessions can easily slip away from us, and people will fail, and things do not satisfy. In Psalm 37 we read that, "I was young and now I am old, yet I have never seen the righteous forsaken or their children begging bread" (Ps. 37:25). As we are abiding in God's dwelling place, it does not mean that there will be no trials. They may come at us on all sides, but they cannot disturb our peace as long as we abide in Him!

Remember, the Lord is at hand! The Lord is strong and mighty. The name of the Lord is a strong tower; the righteous run to it and are safe. Another promise for us is "The eternal God is your refuge and underneath are the everlasting arms" (Deut. 33:27).

Doesn't that make you feel secure? Another comforting verse

in that same chapter is "Let the beloved of the Lord rest secure in him, for he shields him all day long, and the one the Lord loves rests between his shoulders" (Deut. 33:12). Beloved, His love is as unchanging as ever, and He desires that we trust and depend on Him that we might live in peace and be free from anxiety. We must as believers be totally submissive to the will of God in our lives if we are going to find peace. Peace will come to us as we rest in the Lord Jesus Christ.

The Psalmist has said,

> One thing I ask of the Lord, this is what I seek: that I may dwell in the house of the Lord all the days of my life, to gaze upon the beauty of the Lord and to seek Him in His temple. For in the day of trouble He will keep me safe in His dwelling; He will hide me in the shelter of His tabernacle and set me high upon a rock. Then my head will be exalted above the enemies who surround me; at His tabernacle will I sacrifice with shouts of joy; I will sing and make music to the Lord. (Ps. 27:4–6)

Every child of God is a new creation in Christ Jesus, and no other man can fulfill that which God has planned for you. There are no two things alike. Your personality is different from anyone else. He shapes and orders your life that it might influence just the right people. If you live a godly life you will be unpopular and you will be persecuted, but we are to remain unshakeable. That is going to require abstinence from selfishness and self-centeredness. Allow God to use you for noble purposes, for He is worthy of our very best. Paul was able to do that even though he was in chains. He endured hardship for the Lord for there were many obstacles in his path but Paul remained faithful for he knew that everything that came to him had to come through the hand of the Lord Jesus Christ first. His life was hidden with Christ in God. Beloved, tap into that life of power and say, "Surely goodness and love will follow me all the days of my life, and I will dwell in the house of the Lord forever" (Ps. 23:6). Allow the Holy Spirit to control your life for then you will be able to say, "A mighty fortress is my God!" The enemy won't be able to get to you as you hide in that fortress, and the victory will be won. He is the great Protector!

CHAPTER 12

THE PRAYING PROPHET

God had to have a man of courage to speak for Him at the time Ahab and Jezebel sat on the throne of Israel. Elijah was that man, and he was ready. He is probably the greatest prophet in scripture. In 1 Kings, Elijah appeared in the court before Ahab and Jezebel and made a very brave announcement, "As the Lord, the God of Israel lives, whom I serve, there will be neither dew nor rain in the next few years except at my word" (1 Kings 17:1). After this shocking statement, he turned and walked out. We are told in the scriptures that it was a time of apostasy and peril in the nation. Evil forces antagonistic to God and to the worship of God were at work in the court and among the people. Elijah had experienced answered prayer. He knew God's Word and believed it, so he went before King Ahab well assured that God would do exactly what He said. They must have been stunned that this man could speak so boldly.

The secret of Elijah's praying is found in his words, "whom I serve." God was a reality to him. He knew Him as the living God, and he lived in fellowship with Him. He knew that God had told his people,

> If you faithfully obey the commands I am giving
> you today ... to love the Lord your God and to serve
> Him with all your heart and with all your soul ...
> then I will send rain on your land in its season, both
> autumn and spring rains, so that you may gather in
> your grain, new wine and oil. I will provide grass
> in the fields for your cattle, and you will eat and be
> satisfied. Be careful, or you will be enticed to turn
> away and worship other gods and bow down to
> them. Then the Lord's anger will burn against you,
> and He will shut the heavens so that it will not rain
> and the ground will yield no produce, and you will
> soon perish from the good land the Lord is giving
> you. (Deut. ll:l3–17)

Since the people had disobeyed and turned away to worship idols,
Elijah knew God would close the heavens as He had said. So he
prayed earnestly that it might not rain, and it didn't rain on the
land for three and a half years. We see his prayers had the power
to stay the mighty course of nature. We can know what real prayer
is by looking at this prophet. James tells us that Elijah was a man
just like us; a very normal person and God used him mightily. Why
aren't we experiencing more answered prayer? We still have the same
mighty God.

Famine was now in the critical stage in the land. Much of the
vegetation had dried up and the cattle could no longer find places
to graze. King Ahab blamed Elijah for the problem in the land,
so Elijah challenged Ahab to a contest between himself and the
prophets of Baal. We see all the people assembled at Carmel, and it
was quite a contest.

Elijah knew the true hearts of the people. They were pretending
to worship God, but they were also worshiping Baal. As recorded
in I Kings,

Elijah went before the people and said, "How long will you

waver between two opinions? If the Lord is God, follow Him; but if Baal is God, follow him." But the people said nothing. Then Elijah said to them, "I am the only one of the Lord's prophets left, but Baal has four hundred and fifty prophets. Get two bulls for us. Let them choose one for themselves, and let them cut it into pieces and put it on the wood but do not set fire to it. I will prepare the other bull and put it on the wood but not set fire to it. Then you call on the name of your god, and I will call on the name of the Lord. The god who answers by fire ... he is God." (1Kings 18:21–24)

The prophets of Baal put on quite a performance. They begin to call on Baal and nothing happens. They kept crying out, and cut themselves and still nothing. Elijah really enjoyed this spectacle and called out; it may be that Baal has gone on vacation, or maybe he's taking a nap, or why don't you yell a little louder? Then Elijah called all the people to him. He repaired the altar of the Lord that was broken down. He used twelve stones according to the number of tribes in Israel. Then he made a trench, and after preparing the bullock and the wood, he said, "Fill four barrels with water and pour it on the burnt sacrifice, and on the wood" (1 Kings 18:33). They poured water on it three times. Now only the living God can do the impossible. He stepped forward and prayed,

> O Lord, God of Abraham, Isaac and Israel, let it be known today that you are God in Israel and that I am your servant and have done all these things at your command. Answer me, O Lord, answer me, so these people will know that you, O Lord are God, and that you are turning their hearts back again. Then the fire fell and burned up the sacrifice, the wood, the stones and the soil, and also licked up the water in the trench. When the people saw this, they fell prostrate and cried, "The Lord — He is God! The Lord — He is God!" (I Kings 18:36–39)

Elijah's praying turned a whole nation back to God. His praying was strong, insistent and persistent. As he prayed once again on Mount Carmel, the rains finally came. The mighty forces of evil had been defeated, and God won the victory! Beloved, nothing is impossible with the living God!

CHAPTER 13

GUIDANCE

Why is it that so many of us limit God in what He will do for us? As we study the scriptures, we see how the Lord loves to work in impossible situations. He rolled back the Red Sea to let the children of Israel go across on dry ground, He led Noah to build an ark to the saving of his whole family. He closed the mouths of hungry lions when Daniel was thrown into the lion's den, the Hebrew children didn't even smell of smoke when they came out of the fiery furnace. Jonah was spared after spending three days and nights in the belly of a big fish. Do you ever think, "Well I know He can, but will He do this thing for me?" There is a wonderful promise for guidance in Proverbs 3:5–6, "Trust in the Lord with all your heart, and lean not unto your own understanding; in all your ways acknowledge Him, and He will your paths straight". The steps of a good man are ordered by the Lord, and also the stops! Elijah is a true example of this.

We can learn a lot from the life of Elijah and how God directed him when there was a famine in the land. The Lord spoke to Elijah and told him to leave and go east of the Jordan and hide in a ravine of Kerith. He said to stay there for He had ordered the ravens to feed him. They brought him bread and meat every morning and evening, and he drank from the brook. Sometime later the brook dried up for there had been no rain in the land. I'm sure that he could see that the water was going down a little each day and he must have wondered how long he could make it without starving to death or dying of thirst. If Elijah had not been listening to God he could have missed his orders to move on. Isn't it interesting that Elijah didn't have to miss one meal because he waited patiently on God to tell him when to leave the brook? What if he had gone on a few days earlier, or if he had said, "Is that really God speaking and telling me to get out of here?" Then we hear God speaking to him again. This time he is to go to a widow in Zarephath of Sidon. He had commanded this woman to supply Elijah with food for as long as he would stay there.

Elijah obeyed the Lord and went to the town gate and he found the widow gathering sticks. He called to her and asked,

> "Would you bring me a little water in a jar, so I may have a drink?" As she was going to get it, he called, "And bring me, please a piece of bread." "As surely as the Lord your God lives," she replied, "I don't have any bread – only a handful of flour in a jar and a little oil in a jug. I am gathering a few sticks to take home and make a meal for myself and my son that we may eat it – and die." (1 Kings 17:10–12)

There is no record of Elijah's complaining to God. He might have said, "Well God, you must have made a mistake this time for that woman doesn't have enough for me." No, Elijah believed God! He trusted Him to supply his needs. He knew what God had promised. In Psalm 37:5 David said, "I was young and now I am old, yet I have never seen the righteous forsaken or their children begging bread." Over and over the Lord says that He will help us. He will take care of the physical, the material and our spiritual needs just as He did for his prophet.

45

Elijah said to her, "Don't be afraid. Go home and do as you have said. But first make a small cake of bread for me from what you have and bring it to me and then make something for yourself and your son. For this is what the Lord, the God of Israel says: 'The jar of flour will not be used up and the jug of oil will not run dry until the day the Lord gives rain on the land.'" (1 Kings 17:13–14)

Look how the Lord had prepared that woman's heart to obey. She went away and did as Elijah had told her, so there was food every day for Elijah, and for the woman and her son. The jar of flour was not used up, and the jug of oil did not run dry, in keeping with the word of the Lord spoken by Elijah the prophet.

Don't you know that Elijah and the widow were singing praises to God as they stuck their heads into that flour barrel each day and found the handful of meal and little bit of oil that they needed for the day! Now God could have filled that barrel up with meal, but He didn't. He was training His prophet to depend on Him.

Elijah had to have a sacrificial spirit for he knew what would happen when God held back the rain. He was going to have to suffer loss with the rest of the people, but he was willing so that the people might come back to the living and true God. The Lord did use Elijah to show His power in the land while teaching His servant that he could totally depend on Him.

In the book of James we read,

The prayer of a righteous man is powerful and effective. Elijah was a man just like us. He prayed earnestly that it would not rain, and it did not rain on the land for three and a half years. Again he prayed, and the heavens gave rain, and the earth produced its crops. The eyes of the Lord gaze throughout the earth to strengthen those whose hearts are fully committed to Him. (James 5:16–18)

Beloved, God is looking for men and women today who will trust Him to guide them in their everyday walk and with every need they may have.

CHAPTER 14

A TIME OF REFRESHING

Do you feel that you are unloved, rejected, unneeded, and totally unappreciated? Your opinions and suggestions are ignored. Perhaps you feel like a spiritual cripple with no usefulness ahead. Satan knows when you are down, and he delights in hammering away at you to keep you from being a radiant Christian. He would love to destroy your faith and keep you from a holy walk. Take hope! God has not forgotten you. He has not hidden His face from you. In Psalm 22:24 we read, "For he has not despised or disdained the suffering of the afflicted one; he has not hidden his face from him but has listened to his cry for help."

Elijah did a very strange thing after his great victory on Mount Carmel. Ahab reported to Jezebel that Elijah had slain all her prophets of Baal. She was furious with him and sent a message to Elijah threatening to kill him. After standing before the king and all the people, he lost his courage over the threat of one woman and began to run. He kept running until he went into the wilderness, dropped down under a juniper tree, and prayed that he might die. He had enough and asked the Lord to take his life. Elijah was evidently suffering from nervous exhaustion. He was physically and mentally depleted. This just didn't seem to be the same man that defied the prophets of Baal, and as tugged as he was this prophet needed rest. An angel of the Lord touched him and told him to get up and eat. He had nourishing food and drink again and plenty of sleep. It was a time of refreshing for Elijah after the mountain top experience.

We are emotional beings and must come aside to rest our weary minds and bodies. Today's fast lane lifestyle is taxing and we face many emergencies and perplexing situations. We all have our pressure points. In order to live a life that is well pleasing to the Lord, we must come aside at times to rest. We need to retreat to a quiet place away from the daily pressures and distractions that we might refocus on God and His character. We will come away strengthened and able to reach out to others. Then we will be able then to tell our family, friends and neighbors just what Jesus means to us personally and what He can mean to them.

David was able to write the twenty-third Psalm after life had beaten, and battered him. He had experienced the loving, tender care of his Lord. He had felt like running away from it all many times, but he knew that didn't solve his problems. He had to learn to put his trust in the Lord, rest in Him and wait patiently upon Him. When he said, "The Lord is my shepherd, I shall not be in want" (vs. 1), he had tried and proven Him many times. "He makes me lie down in green pastures, he leads me beside quiet waters" (vs. 2). What a comforting thought. David was at rest. "He restores my soul" (vs 3). He was being refreshed and restored. He goes on to say, "Even though I walk through the valley of the shadow of death, I will fear no evil, for you are with me; your rod and your staff, they comfort me" Vs. 4). Even when we are faced with death, He promises that His grace is sufficient, and David found it to be true. He knew that God would provide for him in every way. Beloved, each one of our lives can be used as a powerful tool in the hand of God. He wants us to feel His joy and peace. The Holy Spirit works in mysterious ways to comfort and encourage those in need. As we are edified and comforted, God will be glorified. As we come aside for a time of refreshing, we will be equipped for greater spiritual growth and service, which will make a difference for Christ. We need to be making a difference in this ever changing world.

So many Christians are discouraged because sin, wickedness, and perversion seem to be on the increase everywhere one looks. It is as if darkness has come in like a flood to engulf everything in its path. Sometimes the pressures of life are so intense; it is easy to think that they are going to overwhelm us. We cannot run away from it or just turn around and hope it will go away. No matter how dark things may appear, we know that in the end, Christ will have the victory. The apostle Paul experienced much gloom and darkness when he was thrown into a Roman prison. But God never wastes anything, for out of that period came the truths of the grace of God, the love of the Lord Jesus Christ, and the joy and peace that we can enjoy in any circumstance.

The most vulnerable point in your life as a Christian is right after you've experienced a mighty victory. It is wonderful to have these mountain top experiences. We never want to leave them, but afterwards there is always the valley.

How do you react to the valley experiences? In just a few hours Elijah went from holy boldness, assurance and authority at Mount Carmel to panic, fear, despair and confusion! Are you sitting under a juniper tree filled with discouragement and despair? The enemy will always come at you in your time of greatest blessing. He doesn't want you to be used in the kingdom and will do everything in his power to discourage you. God has told us in James 4:8 to "Submit yourselves, then, to God. Resist the devil, and he will flee from you." After Elijah had been refreshed, he was given anointing power to go out again. He had heard the Word of the Lord and was equipped with strength to obey Him.

We all have these valley experiences in life. The Lord wants to use them, so that we might come out encouraged and refreshed.

You will be richly rewarded as you come aside and allow the Lord to minister to you. We have been called to a lifetime commitment of courage and faithfulness in the service of the Lord. Let us not limit His power, nor doubt His faithfulness, nor grieve His love. He will surely meet our every need.

CHAPTER 15

How to Pray

E very generation has a need to experience the power of God at work in a world that is filled with turmoil and violence. God is waiting for His people to call upon Him, for He does nothing except through the response of the believers. The resources that are available for the believer in Jesus are tremendous. There are riches that this world cannot comprehend. When we are abiding in Him we can go to the Bank of Heaven; a bank that is full of wealth. Citizen of Heaven, do you realize that you can draw on this remarkable bank account, and it will never be overdrawn? Earthly banks may close their doors and fail but not this one, for it has unlimited funds. Why then aren't we using it more? God delights in blessing His people and remember He has said, "You may ask me anything in my name, I will do it" (John 14:14).

> Ask, and it will be given to you; seek and you will find; knock and the door will be opened to you. For everyone who asks receives; he who seeks finds; and to him who knocks, the door will be opened. (Matt. 7:7)

As we pray in the name of Jesus, the power of God is released and people everywhere will be blessed.

To pray according to God's will means to pray in a way that is consistent with the principles in the Word. As you submit your requests to Him, believe that His will is being done according to the greatness of His power and wisdom. As we pray in this manner, we will experience revival in our own life, an intensified awareness of God's near presence, and an eagerness to hear and read the Word. Beloved, live your life to please Jesus and you will have power as you go to Him in prayer. That doesn't mean that we have to be perfect, but as Christians we are to be continually growing in Christ-likeness.

In the 12th chapter of Acts we have a record of a remarkable prayer that the church prayed for Peter when he was in prison. They prayed without ceasing, intensely and unitedly unto God. There was a definite request for Peter that he would be released. This is the kind of praying that brings our Lord into the problem. It is the kind that will release the power of the Holy Spirit upon us. Humanly speaking, there was no hope for Peter. He was guarded by sixteen soldiers and chained by the wrist to a guard on each side of him while they slept. This was truly an impossible situation for him, but as the church met and prayed, God heard and sent an angel. That night while Peter slept, the angel of the Lord touched him and raised him up. The chains fell off and the angel led him out past all the guards and through the iron gate that opened to them of its own accord. Isn't that a miraculous answer to united prayer? There were no divisions in that church group for they had set themselves to prevail in prayer. These believers were praying with fervor and passion, and the Lord was truly in their midst.

Doubt, anxiety, fear and worry focus primarily on circumstances, but faith focuses primarily on God. Doubt and anxiety will try to get you to worry and brood about your problems and needs. Some of life's most valuable lessons are learned by persevering through difficulties. We may never know the true strength of our faith unless it is stretched to the limit. No matter how impossible the situation, you pray God will give you hope as your eyes of faith turn to Him and His promises. Faith sees that He is deeply interested and realizes that all things are possible through prayer. Let us remember Abraham, Jacob, Joseph or Moses who did not waver through unbelief, for they knew that the God of Israel had the power to do what He had promised.

We should spend much time in praise and worship. I believe that we would see many more answers to prayer if we would do as the Psalmist and sing praises to the Lord. There is no doubt that the praise of God's people has opened many iron gates and broken strongholds that have kept the saints bound and defeated. As you praise the Lord, remember to thank Him for the victory.

Prayer takes many forms and serves many spiritual needs. From the formal invocation to the silent cry of a broken heart, prayer enables us to reach out and grasp the outstretched hand of our Creator. God promises much to those who lift their needs to Him. Ask in faith and expect an answer! Deal with any doubt. When you ask God for help, remember that He is faithful. When Jesus invited Peter to walk with Him on the water, Peter was able to do it. That is as long as he kept his eyes on Jesus and stood on His Word. The minute he stopped looking at the Master and focused on his circumstances he began to sink. When you ask God for your needs, focus on the Word and what He is speaking to your heart to believe, rather than letting your faith be determined by your situation. Endure and don't lose heart. Remember that He is not limited by your complicated circumstances. Be persistent and keep praising Him for the answer.

As we wait patiently on the Lord, this process of endurance will build the character we need, in order to receive all that God has prepared for us. Each situation we emerge from in triumph is a small picture of the victory that awaits all believers someday, when we receive the crown of life, which the Lord has promised to those who love Him!

CHAPTER 16

VICTORY

God brought His people through the long journey in the wilderness to the very brink of the Promised Land. Yet, in spite of all their great deliverances and victories, Israel refused to have a settled confidence in God. They said that it was hopeless, that God must have brought them out of Egypt to be destroyed by their enemies. Moses reminded them that in every trial God had shown Himself to be their Deliverer. He had protected them from the plagues, and met all their needs. Moses reminded them that God had never once failed them. Why won't you trust Him to deliver you? How many miracles must He perform before you will trust Him in your next crisis?

You may wonder why they could refuse to trust God after all they had experienced on their journey, but dear saint, don't we react in the same way when we fail to trust the Lord? We miss out on so many victories and blessings when we do not believe God. Let us learn that in all the hard places and strange circumstances that we may be in, He is there with us and makes the opportunities for us to exercise faith that will move mountains of difficulties. God knows how to turn the way of the wicked to a victory for Christ!

King Asa of Judah was a great man of prayer. The revival that came to the nation came because he took away the idols and the high places. He commanded Judah to seek the Lord. Israel had been without a teaching priest and the Word of God for a long time; however, they knew what to do when trouble came. They had been at peace for some time when one day the Cushites marched out against them with a vast army and three hundred chariots. Asa went out to meet him with his brave fighting men, but they were greatly outnumbered. The king called to the Lord his God and said,

> Lord there is no one like you to help the powerless against the mighty. Help us, O Lord our God, for we rely on you, and in your name we have come against this vast army. O Lord, you are our God; do not let man prevail against you. (2 Chron. 14:11)

It seemed impossible that they could hold their own with such a multitude, but his hope was in God. We are told that the Lord struck down the Cushites before Asa and Judah. God gave them a great military victory. All Israel had to do was to gather up the spoil.

There are many times when our burden basket is so full that we think help is impossible. When difficulties come, Jesus has said to cast them all upon Him. Christ is our Victor. As we pray in the name of Jesus, we can loose on earth doors that are closed to the gospel, and hearts that are sealed to Christ. We are appealing to Him who opens doors that no man can shut, and who shuts doors that no man can open.

One main reason for the lack of victory in the church today is the spirit of apathy. There is indifference toward the things of God that is deplorable. God's children do not desire power and victory in their lives enough to really pursue it. This is being spiritually lazy, and we know this is displeasing to God. We lack the strength or desire that will cause us to put on the whole armor of God. We desperately need this protection so that we might be able to withstand all the forces of evil that are keeping us from possessing all God has for us. Have faith in God's Word that tells us that He has delivered us from the power of darkness and has translated us into the kingdom of His dear Son.

There is a thrilling account of a battle won through praise in 2 Chronicles 20. The people of Judah came together to seek help from the Lord. King Jehoshaphat was told that a great multitude was corning against him. He was alarmed and called a fast for Judah. Jehoshaphat stood up in the assembly and after praising God said, "— we have no power to face this great army that is attacking us. We do we know what to do, but our eyes are on you" (2 Chron. 20:12). God spoke through one of the men and said,

> The battle is not yours, but God's. Tomorrow march down against them. ... You will not have to fight this battle. Take your positions; stand firm and see the deliverance the Lord will give you, O Judah and Jerusalem. Do not be afraid; do not be discouraged. Go out to face them tomorrow and the Lord will be with you. (2 Chron. 20:15–17)

They fell down in worship before the Lord, and then they stood up and praised the Lord with a very loud voice. As they sang, the Lord set ambushes against the enemy, and they were defeated! All the men of Judah returned joyfully to Jerusalem and went to the temple of the Lord with harps, flutes and trumpets. The fear of the Lord came upon all the kingdoms of the surrounding countries when they heard how the Lord had fought against the enemies of Israel. And the kingdom of Jehoshaphat was at peace, for his God had given them the victory!

If there is a great trial in your life today, do not be defeated, but continue by faith to claim the victory through Him who is able to make you more than a conqueror. When the enemy comes in like a flood, it may seem for a while that he will win, but the Lord has promised to lift up a standard against him. Keep hanging in and a glorious victory will soon be apparent.

fallen on Judah and Jerusalem, and God had made them an object of dread, horror and scorn.

The king reminded the people that the Assyrians had already taken some of them into captivity. Hezekiah told them that he intended to make a covenant with the Lord so that His fierce anger would turn away from them. They listened and obeyed the instructions of Hezekiah. The nation had fallen so far from God that many of them had been without the Word all their lives. When they assembled and consecrated themselves, they went in to purify the temple. King Hezekiah gathered the officials together and went up to the temple. The priests made the sin offering for all Israel, and the Levites entered the temple with cymbals, harps and lyres. As the offering began, they started singing accompanied by trumpets and other instruments. The whole assembly bowed in worship. It was really an exciting time for Judah. The service of the temple was reestablished, and all the people rejoiced at what God had brought about in such a short time.

Hezekiah invited all Israel to come to Jerusalem so that they might celebrate the Feast of Unleavened Bread. They all came to the celebration and ate even though many had not been purified according to what was in the law.

> Hezekiah prayed for them, saying, "May the Lord, who is good, pardon everyone who sets his heart on seeking God — the Lord, the God of his fathers — even if he is not clean according to the rules of the sanctuary." And the Lord heard Hezekiah and healed the people. (2 Chron. 30:18–19)

The festival lasted seven days. They had such a wonderful time that they extended it for another week. There was great joy in in that city. Since the time of Solomon, there had not been anything like it.

When Hezekiah went into Judah as king, he changed the kingdom. He was not only a man of faith but also a man of prayer.

He was greatly blessed by having the prophet Isaiah for his friend and counselor. God tests and trains all his children, and after all the wonderful blessings, there came a very troublesome time for this great man. Assyria was at the very gate of Jerusalem and ready to make an attack. They began by terrifying the people. The king did all that he could to fortify the city, but he was trusting God to help him when he told his people,

> Be strong and courageous. Do not be afraid or discouraged because of the king of Assyria and the vast army with him, for there is a greater power with us than with him. With him is only the arm of flesh, but with us is the Lord our God to help us and to fight our battles. (2 Chron. 32:7–8).

The people rested themselves upon the word of Hezekiah. After the king had encouraged the people to trust the Lord, we are told that he and Isaiah prayed and cried to the Lord. They depended upon the Lord for help, and the Almighty delivered the city in a miraculous way.

Some years later Hezekiah became ill and was at the point of death.

> The prophet Isaiah ... went to him and said, "This is what the Lord says: Put your house in order because you will die; you will not recover." Hezekiah turned his face to the wall and prayed to the Lord, "Remember O Lord how I have walked before you faithfully and with wholehearted devotion and have done what is good in your eyes". Hezekiah wept bitterly. Before Isaiah had left the middle court, the word of the Lord came to him: "Go back and tell Hezekiah, the leader of my people, 'this is what the Lord, the God of your father David, says: I have

> heard your prayer and seen your tears; I will heal you. On the third day from now you will go up to the temple of the Lord. I will add fifteen years to your life, and I will deliver you and this city from the hand of the king of Assyria. I will defend this city for my sake and for the sake of my servant David.'" (2 Kings 20:1–6)

Isaiah told him to take a lump of figs and lay it on the boil, and then he recovered. This was a remarkable answer to prayer

We all need to trust the Lord as Hezekiah did in times of calamity that come as a result of divine judgment. As these judgments take place before our very eyes, your only answer is to have Jesus as your shield. Run today to meet Him in the secret closet of prayer. Know that "the Lord is a refuge for the oppressed, a stronghold in times of trouble. Those who know your name will trust in you, for you Lord, have never forsaken those who seek you" (Ps 9:9–10). Christ must be vitally real to us if we are to remain faithful to Him in the hour of crisis.

CHAPTER 18

THE PRAYER OF A RIGHTEOUS MAN

W hat does it mean to be a righteous person? James has told us that the prayer of a righteous man is powerful and effective. Elijah was called a righteous man and he had power in prayer to close the heavens over his whole country! He goes on to say that he was a man just like us. God yearns to show us His power and strength in our day, and He is looking for men and women that He can work through. The Lord spoke to Ezekiel and said, "I looked for a man among them who would build up the wall and stand before me in the gap on behalf of the land so I would not have to destroy it, but I found none" (Ezek. 22:30). What a sad state that nation was in. Have we realized just how important it is to be able to stand in the gap for the Lord and for leadership that will call the people of God to prayer? We know that prayer is definite work, as much so as preaching is a work of the Lord.

We need to have our minds opened to the possibilities of prayer, and to set ourselves to seek the kingdom of God and His righteousness, so that we can pray like Elijah. He knew God. He knew the will of God, so he could pray the prayer that prevailed for

Israel. The work of prayer requires knowledge of the Word. God has promised that if we ask anything according to His will He hears us.

Old Testament history is filled with accounts of praying saints. No matter how far away from God Israel drifted, no matter how they fell; their cry to God always brought deliverance. They were ever learning yet forgetting that prayer always brought God to their deliverance, for there was nothing too hard for God to do for His people. All of the saints were in extreme difficulties at times, but nothing but prayer could deliver them. The sun stood still and the moon stayed until the people had avenged themselves on their enemies as Joshua prayed. Prayer was the mighty force that brought unfaithful Jonah from the belly of the fish. God rescued him despite his sin of fleeing from duty. The united prayers of the praying king and the praying prophet were mighty forces in bringing deliverance and defeating God's enemies in Hezekiah's reign.

Make every effort to live in peace with all men and to be holy, without holiness no one will see the Lord. God disciplines us for our good that we may share in His holiness. No discipline seems pleasant at the time, but painful. Later on, however, it produces a harvest of righteousness and peace for those who have been trained by it. Beloved, to be righteous is to live a life that is pleasing to the Lord, to lay down any sin, confess it to the Lord, and accept His forgiveness and cleansing. Paul believed that a holy life changes a person's focus, and could say that "Sin shall not be master over you" (Rom. 6:14).

David said in Psalm 119, "Blessed are they whose ways are blameless, who walk according to the law of the Lord. Blessed are they who keep his statutes and seek him with all their heart" (Ps 119:1–2). Luke speaks of Zacharias and his wife Elizabeth as both being righteous before God, walking in all the commandments and ordinances of the Lord blameless. In Proverbs we are told that if we set our sight to walk blameless before God, we will walk in His favor. God will give the righteous a good name, so they can use it to glorify Him in greater measure. "And the work of righteousness shall be peace; and the effect of righteousness quietness and assurance forever" (Isa. 32:17 NKJV).

Why aren't the righteous praying more today? The Hebrew children called and God delivered them from the fiery furnace. God's power has an effect over every force in the universe. It doesn't matter if it is wild tigers and lions or exceedingly wicked people which are all around us. If we weren't kept by the power of God and His angels, none of us would last very long. Are we too busy to intercede at such a time as this?

Beloved, difficult days are coming on the earth and God is looking for righteous men and women to stand in the gap. May the Lord conform us more to His image, as we study His Word. May our prayer of faith move Almighty God as we bow in humble submission to His perfect will.

CHAPTER 19

HINDRANCES TO PRAYER

"Your sins have hidden his face from you, so that he will not hear" (Isa. 59:1) said Isaiah to Israel. Therefore, when prayer is unanswered, you need to ask, "Is there anything in my life that is hindering God from answering my prayer? Am I regarding iniquity in my heart?"

According to the Word, it is sin in us and not the unwillingness of God to hear our prayers, for we are told "Your iniquities have separated you from your God, and your sins have hidden his face from you" (Isa. 59:2). There is an excellent word from David when he prayed, "Search me O God, and know my heart; test me and know my anxious thoughts. See if there be any offensive way in me" (Ps. 139:23). It is good then to wait before the Lord and see if He can put His finger upon anything in your life. The only way to find true peace is to confess the sin and then forsake it. Sin is an awful thing for it will break our fellowship with the Father.

In so many instances we may pray selfishly, or there could be an unforgiving spirit within our heart. There can be a lack of love. In I Peter 3 we see that a wrong relationship between husband and wife is a hindrance to prayer. Many prayers are hindered by unbelief. "That man should not think that he will receive anything from the Lord" (James 1:7). Stinginess is another sin, "If a man shuts his ears to the cry of the poor, he too will cry out and not be answered" (Proverbs 21:13).

We are hindered by spiritual enemies. We are instructed to,

> Be strong in the Lord and in his mighty power. Put on the full armor of God so that you can take your stand against the devil's schemes. For our struggle is not against flesh and blood, but against the rulers, against the authorities, against the powers of this dark world and against the spiritual forces of evil in the heavenly realms. Therefore put on the full armor of God so that when the day of evil comes, you may be able to stand your ground, and after you have done everything, to stand. {Eph. 6:10–13)

The evidence of a spiritual enemy is well illustrated in the 10th chapter of Daniel. He had been praying and no answer had come. Finally an angel came and touched him and said,

> Do not be afraid, Daniel. Since the first day that you set your mind to gain understanding, and to humble yourself before your God, your words were heard, and I have come in response to them. But the prince of the Persian kingdom resisted me twenty-one days. Then Michael, one of the chief princes, came to help me, because I was detained there with the king of Persia. (Dan. 10:12–13)

This was a spiritual battle that was going on, and we too are having them. We don't seem to realize that spiritual warfare being carried on today. People need to be grounded in the Word of God in order to be able to stand. The battle is carried on wherever the Word of God is preached and the gospel is given out.

Are we praying enough for our pastors as they teach the Word? We should be upholding their hands as Aaron and Hur upheld the hands of Moses on behalf of Israel. We need to take our stand with them and fight these battles.

> Stand firm then, with the belt of truth buckled around your waist, with the breastplate of righteousness in place, and with your feet fitted with the readiness that comes from the gospel of peace. In addition to all this, take up the shield of faith, with which you can extinguish all the flaming arrows of the evil one. Take the helmet of salvation and the sword of the Spirit, which is the word of God. (Eph. 6:14–17)

Dear saints, are you overwhelmed by a satanic attack? In the little book of James he tells us to

> Submit yourselves, then, to God. Resist the devil, and he will flee from you. Come near to God and He will come near to you ... Humble yourselves before the Lord, and He will lift you up. (James 4:7–10)

Remember the Lord often said, "I am with you." He is your strength! No matter what Satan may bring against you, you can stand in His victory and power! Keep on praying. Never give up. God answers prayer. Pray without ceasing!

CHAPTER 20

THE PATH TO MATURITY

God's plan for our lives is that we will be conformed into the image of His Own Dear Son, the Lord Jesus Christ. In our spiritual life, God often has to wake us up by the presence of trying circumstances, which forces us into new places of trust. We are just like a plant that needs both the sunshine and rain. We can't grow spiritually without testings and trials.

There is a beautiful promise in Psalm 37:4, "Delight yourself in the Lord; and He will give you the desires of your heart." As we become more like Him, His thoughts become our thoughts. Our prayers shall be in accord with His will, and bring back to us the desires of our heart, which are actually His desires. As we grow spiritually, it is so natural for our goals to change.

We will want to grow in godliness. Just reading the Bible through three times doesn't always make one mature in the faith. However, there are believers today who regularly shut themselves in with God. They are getting to know Him. That intimacy is giving birth to great trust! We definitely need to be mature citizens of heaven. If we are not, it will be most difficult in the perilous times that are ahead. If we are overcome with fear, terror, and hopelessness, we will lose our song of victory. This is why we need to grow spiritually.

Daniel's heart was filled with God's love for His work and kingdom, and his prayers were powerful forces. Anything allowed in the heart which is contrary to the will of God, let it seem ever so insignificant, or ever so hidden; will cause us to fall before our enemies. We should be so careful that there is no root of bitterness in our heart toward another. Disobedience in our life any one of these things will bring defeat, and cause us to go into spiritual decline. God wants to see a great demonstration of faith in our lives. Sometimes He has to keep away encouraging results until we learn to trust without them. Then He loves to show the fruits of our labor.

Abraham was brought to the end of his own strength that he might see that in his own body he could do nothing. He had to trust God alone. That is what He wants us to do. May God fill us with His divine love. It is with faith that we believe God desires to raise up a people who will make a difference now and for generations to come!

Paul urges us "not to conform any longer to the pattern of this world, but to be transformed by the renewing of your mind. Then you will be able to test and approve what God's will is — His good, pleasing and perfect will" (Rom. 12:2). Peter says, "But you are a chosen people, a royal priesthood, a holy nation, a people belonging to God, that you may declare the praises of him who called you out of darkness into his wonderful light" (1 Pet. 2:9). There are many Christians who no longer walk in God's favor. They have no power of the Spirit on them. Your holy life will disturb and even repel them. You may be rejected, but dear saint, you will gain favor from God. "Let love and faithfulness never leave you; bind them around your neck, write them on the tablet of your heart. Then you will win favor and a good name in the sight of God and man" (Proverbs 3:3–4). Paul experienced much rejection for when he wrote to Timothy he said,

> At my first defense, no one came to my support, but
> everyone deserted me. May it not be held against
> them. But the Lord stood at my side and gave me
> strength, so that through me the message might
> be fully proclaimed and all the gentiles might hear
> it. And I was delivered from the lion's mouth. The
> Lord will rescue me from every evil attack and will
> bring me safely to his heavenly kingdom. (II Tim.
> 4:16–18)

In order to grow spiritually, we must make peace with the past, forget the negative things, and concentrate on the positive. So often we accept God's forgiveness, but it is so difficult to forgive ourselves. There is so much wasted time grieving over the things we have done. Dig a hole and bury those things! God has cast them into the uttermost part of the sea. He has forgiven and forgotten. Now we must be able to forgive ourselves! Then get on with life and make a contribution to the new life in Christ. Build relationships with the Christians. We need each other and the fellowship of other believers. Become the person God has created you to be. Ditch your druthers and want only the perfect will of God for your life. Get together with those who know how to pray. The fellowship you have controls a lot as to what you become. The benefits are tremendous, and you will have a place of refuge, a shield and joy as you share the things of the Lord. You will also find strength, a true appreciation for spiritual things, and your spirit will yearn for more of the Lord.

The apostle Paul calls us to live a separated life, and warns us about being yoked together with unbelievers. He knew that we would never mature unless we could spend some time with people of like minds. The Scriptures will influence, nourish, and enrich the human spirit.

> The law of the Lord is perfect, reviving the soul.
> The statutes of the Lord are trustworthy, making

wise the simple. The precepts of the Lord are right, giving joy to the heart. The commands of the Lord are radiant, giving light to the eyes. The fear of the Lord is pure enduring forever. (Ps.19:7–9)

My prayer for every believer is that Our Lord will teach us His Word, conform us more to His image, and make us vessels fit for His use as we approach the end of the age.

CHAPTER 21

A THANKFUL HEART

We are admonished in the Word of God to give thanks for all things unto God. In everything give thanks, for this is the will of God concerning you. But how can we do this when we're in serious trouble? When bad things happen it is most difficult to thank God. It seems almost hypocritical to try. But dear saint, we know He who watches over us will take those terrible and even tragic things and somehow work good out of them. We do not have the wisdom to always know whether something is good or bad, and seemingly to us it is bad. But we do know that our Lord is gracious and good. Whatever He permits has to first come through Him. What better time than now to set our hearts to be thankful?

Job suffered greatly and lost everything; his children and all his possessions. His body was covered with boils, his wife was no help, yet he was still able to say "Though he slays me, yet will I hope in him" (Job 13:15). Things were terrible for Job. Even his friends accused him of having sin in his life. Job didn't understand all that was going on about him, but he was still able to trust God. A day finally came when he realized that something good was coming out of his experience.

We are told to enter into His gates with thanksgiving, and into His courts with praise! It is not within the natural man to be thankful for we are much more given to complaints. As we seek that spirit of thanksgiving from the Lord, He will give us a thankful heart. The next time you feel discouraged and full of fear determine to praise the Lord for His goodness, and thank Him for the many blessings in your life. It may help to name them one by one. It will truly amaze you as to what the Lord has done! As you thank Him heartily for each one, see if your spirits stay down. There is no way! You will begin to feel blessed. Before you know it your heart is warmed up, and all the depression has departed! You will be rejoicing and praising God. One of the best places to start is in the Psalm 103 that reads,

> Bless the Lord, O my soul; and all that is within me, bless His holy name! Bless the Lord, O my soul, and forget not all His benefits. Who forgives all your iniquities, who heals all your diseases, who redeems your life from destruction, who crowns you with lovingkindness and tender mercies. (Ps. 103:1 NKJV)

I'm afraid that ingratitude is a prevalent sin in the church today, and it is characteristic of the apostasy spoken of in Timothy. In that little book we are told, "People will be lovers of themselves, lovers of money, boastful ... disobedient to their parents, ungrateful, unholy ... without self-control ... lovers of pleasure rather than lovers of God" (2 Tim. 3:2–9). We are like the ten lepers that came to Jesus and cried for mercy and healing. He healed them all, but nine of the ten didn't appreciate the goodness of God toward them enough to return and offer thanks. They took His blessing for granted and soon forgot what He had done for them.

Moses had to deal with a lot of murmuring and complaining among the people as they wandered through the wilderness. God gave them manna to eat each day. They didn't have to get out and work for it, but they complained because they were tired of it. They longed for the food they had Egypt when they were in slavery. They complained against Moses and Aaron and said they had brought them into the wilderness to kill them with hunger. This was after they had seen all the miracles. It was really speaking against God for they knew that He had kept their clothes from wearing out and met all their other needs.

It is so easy for us to look at their actions and say, "How could they have been so ungrateful?" What about the church today? Do you think that we might have short memories like the Israelites? We will never know on this side of eternity just how much the Lord has spared us. I wonder if we can even realize just how many blessings He has given us. We have enjoyed our freedoms in this country. I can't even imagine how it would be in a nation that would forbid you to own a Bible or to worship God.

God has made it very clear in Psalm 50 that He is not interested in getting any material gift from his children. The whole world belongs to Him. Our heavenly Father is in the giving business. He delights in giving to you and me. There is one thing that He wants, and that is for us to give Him thank offerings.

In Psalm 69:30 David tells us, "I will praise God's name in song and glorify him with thanksgiving. This will please the Lord more than an ox." The sacrifice of thanksgiving was one of the regular sacrifices ordained by God in the book of Leviticus.

Oh, that men would give thanks to the Lord for His goodness, and for His wonderful works to the children of men! Let them sacrifice the sacrifices of thanksgiving, and declare His works with rejoicing. (Ps. 107:21–22).

We are being cheated out of the joy of the Lord because we do not really know Him. He wants us to love Him. Absolute surrender of our desires will help us to realize God's presence. In Psalm 46:10 we find that He is a God at hand, and He tells us "Be still and know that I am God." We must shut ourselves in with the Lord. The better we know Him, the more we love Him.

The first thanksgiving proclamation was made in 1789 by

George Washington. He called the nation to a special day of prayer and thanksgiving to acknowledge that God had given them His protection and a form of government for the safety and happiness of the people. Dear saints, God's people should be filled with expressions of gratitude and thanksgiving every day of the year. The Lord did not ordain praise solely for His benefit, but for ours. When we praise Him, we rehearse all the attributes of a mighty God and the many ways He has worked in our lives. We remind ourselves that God is more powerful than our circumstances, and that makes us joyful.

It's not easy to be thankful to the Lord through terrible circumstances, but the results are certainly worth the effort! God has never failed us yet, so give Him thanks and be joyful. Let everything that has breath give praise and thanksgiving to the Lord!

CHAPTER 22

ENCOURAGEMENT FOR HEAVY HEARTS

I t is always encouraging to hear good news. In today's world, we hear very little that will bring encouragement and cheer. Somehow, the good news never makes the headlines, but the bad or the terrible is what we have all around us. The prophet Habakkuk was living in troublesome times also, yet he was able to walk by faith with God. He knew that God was the answer to the problems of his day. In spite of impending judgment, Habakkuk was able to say, "I will be joyful in God my savior" (Hab. 3:18). The book opens in gloom but ends in a song of glory. May you and I be encouraged today by the Word of God!

God has given us His Word as a compass to guide us through any situation we face. We are to be encouragers to the needy and lead those who are perishing to safety. Jesus said,

> Do not let your heart be troubled; believe in God; believe also in me. In my Father's house are many rooms; if it were not so, I would have told you. I am going there to prepare a place for you. And if I go

and prepare a place for you, I will come back and
take you to be with me that you also may be where
I am. You know the way to the place where I am
going. (John 14:1–4)

A heart at peace gives life to the body and we know that a cheerful
heart is good medicine. But beloved, even in facing death, He who
promises to be our Guide until the end will give us His grace that
is sufficient. He will swallow up death in victory, and He has told
us that "Precious in the sight of the Lord is the death of His saints"
(Ps. 116:15)

How can we encourage ourselves? We read that David
strengthened himself in the Lord. As we look to the Psalms, there are
so many encouraging verses that give hope. He promises to be our
help and shield. One of my favorite Psalms I can go in time of trial is

Have mercy on me, O God, have mercy on me, for
in you my soul takes refuge. I will take refuge in the
shadow of your wings until the disaster has passed.
I cry out to God Most High, to God who fulfills
His purpose for me. (Psalm 57:1–3)

He has promised to be our strength no matter what happens. How
can we be encouraged in that? Psalm 46 tells us that

God is our refuge and strength, and ever present
help in trouble. Therefore we will not fear, though
the earth gives way and the mountains fall into the
heart of the sea, though its waters roar and foam
and the mountains quake with their surging. The
Lord Almighty is with us. (Ps. 46:1–3)

These verses are very comforting. When we are comforted by God,
we should comfort others.

Let your life as a Christian be an inspiration and model for others to see. We are to encourage others and show them how they can align themselves with the Word of God that they might live more meaningful lives. There are so many discouraged people today that need to be uplifted. There are instructions for us dear friends, and they are found in Romans 12. Beloved, love must be sincere. Hate what is evil, cling to what is good. Be devoted to one another in brotherly love. Honor one another above yourselves. Never be lacking in zeal, but keep your spiritual fervor serving the Lord. Be joyful in hope, patient in affliction, faithful in prayer. Share with God's people who are in need. Practice hospitality. Do you think you would find this in the average fellowship today? What then is wrong with God's children? Are we so busy and indifferent that we are ignoring God's admonition to give hope and encouragement to the believers?

In Hebrews 10:24 it says, "And let us consider how to stimulate one another to love and good deeds." We are told why this is so desperately needed. "— in the last days perilous times will come" (2 Timothy 3:1). We will need all the help and encouragement that we can get in order that we keep from falling into discouragement. We need to refrain from the harsh verbal putdowns that so many well-meaning people give out. We can get that out in the market place, and we certainly don't want to be guilty of doing that to our brothers and sisters in Christ.

I can remember once when I was going through a particular trial, and felt as though my world was falling apart, a dear old lady that I hardly knew, wrote me a note to say she wanted me to know she loved me and would be praying. What an encouragement! That was many years ago, but I have never forgotten what a help that was. It caused me to look up to God and to remember what I had in Him. That lady was so full of compassion and thoughtfulness, and I'm sure she helped many people along the way. Look at this,

Praise be to the God and Father of our Lord Jesus Christ, the Father of compassion and the God of all comfort, who comforts us in all our troubles, so that we can comfort those in any trouble with the comfort we ourselves have received from God. (2 Cor. 3:3–4)

You may say, "Well how could I give encouragement to someone today?" God promises to direct our paths and I'm sure there must be friends, relatives, and people at the work place that need a kind word. Just a smile will do wonders at times. But I believe the Lord will direct us to those who may need a visit, a note or a telephone call.

If the world can see the church being what it should be to each other, it will bring revival. They will be seeking after what you have when they see the love, the kindness, the joy, and that precious peace that no one can explain. Let your light shine before men, that they may see your good deeds and praise your Father in heaven.

Beloved, God is calling His people to action, to boldly declare that Jesus Christ is Lord of All, and the only answer to the needs we face today for encouraging heavy hearts.

CHAPTER 23

A MAN OF FAITH

The Word of God tells us that following the Flood and the scattering of the people from the Tower of Babel, God turned to one individual. From that individual He is going to make a nation, give His revelation and bring the Redeemer. God made a covenant with the Father of the Jewish nation that is an everlasting possession. The source of every blessing the Church possesses today.

When He chose Abraham He knew that he was a man of faith. It is amazing how God works and was able to bring this man out of a pagan land that served other gods. He left everything he had known in the Ur of the Chaldees, which was somewhere near the Persian Gulf. When God spoke to him He said,

> Get out of your country, from your family and from your father's house, to a land that I will show you. I will make you a great nation; I will bless you and make your name great; and you shall be a blessing. ... in you all the families of the earth shall be blessed. (Gen. 12:1–3 NKJV)

Abraham believed God, and he went out not knowing where he was going. He didn't even say, "Lord where are you telling me to go?"

All the Lord had to do was point him in the right direction and tell him when to start walking. Imagine the long, hot journey he faced. He had Sarah his wife, his nephew Lot, and many others with him. Wherever they stopped to rest for the night, Abraham erected an altar and called upon the Lord. That was his testimony to God. He quietly worshiped Him, and the Canaanites soon learned this about him. God surely had a plan and a purpose for Abraham and for his people, and for Israel in the future. We can almost hear Abraham saying, "I delight to do your will, O my God; your law is within my heart" (Psalm 40:8). We are never told that he questioned God but followed Him every step of the way. We may ask ourselves what kind of a testimony I have.

Abraham is considered to be one of the greatest men who ever lived. He stands as a man of noble character and well known all over the world. Judaism, Islam and Christianity all claim him. In our day of television and radio people in Asia and all over Africa have heard of Abraham. The scriptures tell us that he believed God and did not waver in unbelief. He continued following his God even when things were tough. As you study his life, you soon discover that he was far from perfect. In fact, he made many mistakes, and God never tried to hide this from us. Abraham was never ready to give up when he failed. If he fell in the ditch, he would get up, brush himself off, and start all over again. He learned to trust God as he went through the many trials and difficulties, and he had plenty of them. It takes years sometimes before we learn the things the LORD wants to teach us, for we lose patience and become tired of the struggle and just give up.

Abraham was seventy-five years old when God spoke to him, and he departed on his long journey south. Shortly after they arrived in Canaan, there was a great famine in the land. When he heard that Egypt had plenty of food, he and Sarah decided to leave Canaan and go there. He should have stayed in Canaan until God told him to leave, for he was in the place of blessing. This was his big mistake. Because Sarah was so beautiful, Abraham almost lost her to Pharaoh. When God revealed to Pharaoh that Sarah was Abraham's wife, Pharaoh changed his mind returned her. They also acquired a maid by the name of Hagar while they were there which caused them much heartbreak. When God puts us into a place, He will meet our needs however, Abraham hadn't learned that yet.

When Abraham returned from the land of Egypt, he was very rich in cattle, gold and silver. He and Lot began to have strife with all their herdsmen. They needed more space, so they decided to separate. God had given Abraham all the land, but he was very generous with Lot. He told Lot he could choose whatever he wanted, and he would take what was left. Lot chose the plain of Jordan, which was Sodom, and Abraham stayed in the land of Canaan.

The birth of Isaac was a miraculous birth, for Abraham was one hundred years old and Sarah was ninety. They had waited for the promise of a son for many years. Ishmael had been born to Hagar, the maid. Abraham loved him very much, for he was his son also. They began to have trouble in their household, and Sarah insisted that Ishmael and Hagar must leave. This was a heartbreaking situation, for Abraham wanted Ishmael to share in the promise God had given him for the land. God refused and told him that Isaac was the chosen one. However, God did promise that He would bless Ishmael and make of him a great nation. He has fulfilled this promise. The Arabs are descendants of Ishmael.

Abraham went through many difficult situations in his life, but the greatest crisis was when he was asked by God to give up Isaac as a sacrifice. He did not understand it, for he knew Isaac was the son of the promise God had given him. We are told that Abraham believed God and fully obeyed and trusted Him to raise Isaac from the dead. Isaac was not a small child when this happened. He could have totally rebelled when Abraham was ready to sacrifice him, but he submitted to his father. As Abraham stretched forth his hand and took the knife to slay his son, God spoke to him and said, "Do not lay a hand on the boy" (Gen. 22:12). Had Abraham passed the test? He had been tested before by faith, but now God could see that he trusted Him by his actions.

This was a supreme test for Abraham and God does not have to ask anything more of him. He had proved that God had first place in his life. Dear friend, any person called by the Lord is going to be tried and tested in some way. The tests are given us to strengthen our faith, to build character, and to make us more serviceable for the LORD. He wants us to be lights in this dark world, to be ambassadors until He returns, and to launch out in full faith to proclaim the gospel whenever the opportunity. Proverbs 3:5–6 tells us to "Trust in the LORD with all your heart; do not depend on your own understanding. Seek His will in all you do, and He will direct your paths." The Word of God is filled with promises from the Lord. They are there for you, so start searching and make them yours.

CHAPTER 24

HOPE

Friend, what do you do when you find yourself in a difficult circumstance? What happened when all your joy and happiness has escaped and things look pretty hopeless? David found himself in such a situation. He and all his men came home from a battle to find that the city had been burned and all the women and children had been taken captive. He was greatly distressed and the people were so angry they talked of stoning David. They were all grieved and wept many tears, but we are told in I Samuel 30:6 that David encouraged himself in the Lord. So many times when help seems impossible and the old enemy is around to whisper in your ear that there's no hope; it is tempting to give up. Beloved, the Lord wants to make Himself real to us, and as we study the Psalms we can see that David was writing them through times like these. The Lord is good, and David found this to be true.

Hope decides how we are going to view what is happening about us. When we are without hope, we can go into depression, but what did David do? Everyone in his life let him down, and he had every reason to become bitter, but God gave him hope of better things to come. We know that David suffered many sorrows but we read in Psalm 119:28, "My soul is weary with sorrow; strengthen me according to your word." And in another psalm he said, "I wait for the Lord, my soul waits, and in his Word I put my hope" (Ps. 130:5).

God keeps us depending on Him, and the problems and troubles of everyday life keep us seeking Him. As we look into the word for comfort, God strengthens us. Over and over the psalmist asks himself: "Why are you downcast, O my soul? Why so disturbed within me? Put your hope in God, for I will yet praise Him, my Savior and my God" (Ps. 42:5). He doesn't keep looking inward to try to analyze his problem, but he turns immediately to God and by faith begins to praise Him.

Dear reader, did you know that God is for you and not against you? He loves to stretch our faith and broaden our vision. Part of God's plan for us is to be broken from self-reliance. It is always painful to give up our security blanket. We panic and act just like a little child when we're torn from the familiar things. God may put us through many trials and testings, but He doesn't test us to flunk us. A test is to prove that our faith is genuine. He loves us so much and wants us to grow and mature in every area. In Romans 15:13 we are told, "May the God of hope fill you with all joy and peace as you trust in Him, so that *you* may overflow with hope by the power of the Holy Spirit." What happens when we overflow with hope and joy? Others will be blessed! Our families, friends and the church will benefit.

You may be in a family situation that seems hopeless. You've cried out to God many times and *you* are only hanging on by a thread. You think about running away, but where would you go, and without enough money to take you if you could leave your responsibilities? Well, what do you do? In Psalms we read,

> The righteous cry out, and the Lord hears them; he delivers them from all their troubles. The Lord is close to the brokenhearted and saves those who are crushed in spirit. (Ps. 34:17–18)

Look up to Him in faith and He will carry you through and give you hope.

Jacob ran away from his home and stayed for twenty years. Those were years of heartache and trouble. He eventually had to return and face his brother Esau. God wants us to turn that difficulty over to Him for He is the only one that can bring peace and joy into our lives. Habakkuk had seen much violence and wickedness in the land and he couldn't understand why God had allowed it to continue. God finally spoke to him and told him that He was going to use a nation that was even more wicked to punish Judah. Even though they had many problems, Habakkuk was able to turn in hope to the Lord for he says,

> Though the fig tree does not bud, and there are no grapes on the vines, though the olive crop fails and the fields produce no food, though there are no sheep in the pen and no cattle in the stalls, yet I will rejoice in the Lord. I will be joyful in God my Savior. The Sovereign Lord is my strength, he makes my feet like the feet of a deer, He enables me to go on the heights. (Hab. 3:17–19)

Beloved, He is our hope. We are looking for that blessed hope, and the glorious appearing of the great God and our Savior, Jesus Christ who gave Himself for us to redeem us from all wickedness and to purify for Himself a people that are His very own, eager to do what is good. We have this hope which is an anchor for the soul.

CHAPTER 25

THE GOLDEN YEARS

God has given to us wonderful promises in the scriptures for the "golden years." Even to our old age, He has not forsaken His children, and He has told us that His grace is sufficient regardless of our circumstances. Scripture abounds in promises that await our appropriation. There is no conceivable situation for which there is no appropriate promise.

Be alert as you read the Bible to discover what God has promised to do and then lay hold of it. They must be claimed by faith. It was by faith the patriarchs received the promises. Take hold of the great promises of scripture and step out in confidence.

An American newspaper conducted a survey and discovered the three greatest problems concerning its readers were fear, worry, and loneliness. Loneliness is a scourge for the elderly, not only for the poor but also the rich. Many have lost a mate and friends. Others are suffering with aches and pains along with failing eyesight and deaf ears. How many people would give away their fortunes just to have peace of mind? This has to be mankind's greatest need. There is no way this stressful world can give this kind of peace and rest. The Lord has not only promised to care for us in old age, but gives us the assurance that we can be fruitful. Ps.92 says "The righteous will flourish like a palm tree. They will grow like a cedar of Lebanon planted in the house of the Lord ... they will still bear fruit in old age" (Ps. 92:12–14).

We know that God is never in a hurry with His children, but spends years in teaching and training those He plans to use. Moses was eighty years old before he began his work. He had to spend many years on the back side of the desert before delivering the Israelites from Egypt. Paul wrote in his letter to Titus that the older women were to teach the younger ones to love their families, to be discreet, chaste, keepers at home, good, obedient to their own husbands, that the word of God be not blasphemed. The Lord has promised to give each one of us the strength to do whatever He has called us for, and He has said, "As your days so shall your strength be" (Deut. 33:25). Am I prepared to let God do a work in me that is worthy of Himself? Beloved, there is no limit to what God can do with a holy surrendered life regardless of age.

Isaiah tells us that "Even to your old age and gray hairs I am he, who will sustain you ... and I will rescue you" (Isa. 46:4). One of the greatest ministries for the golden years is intercessory prayer. We should never retire from prayer. It is a full-time job just bringing the needs of the people around us to the Lord. There are such desperate needs today in our families, the churches, our communities, and the nation. He wants us to acknowledge our personal needs as well as all the others. In Psalm 90:12 we read, "Teach us to number our days aright, that we may gain a heart of wisdom." This wisdom that He offers is surely needed as we minister to our children, grand-children, and all others around us. So let us come boldly to the throne of grace that we may obtain mercy, and find grace to help in time of need.

God wants our loved ones to know Him, and as we abide in Him. He will show Himself through us. Do we have the faith to believe for all those He has lain upon our hearts? This is a great and mighty ministry that we can have. As He works through us winning precious souls for Jesus, He also wants to bless and encourage His defeated children. We all need to encourage others for this old noisy, wicked world has forgotten that there is a God in heaven. Let us make them aware that God is still alive and well. He able to bring freedom from fear, worry, and loneliness, for He is the one we go to for that perfect peace and rest. We are to be like springs of living water, but I'm afraid that most Christians are more like stagnant pools. Somehow, we think we are of little value in our world, but as we allow the Holy Spirit to have control, then we will overflow to others. However helpless and incapable we may believe ourselves to be, we can be of service in some way. It may not seem to be any great thing, but only a telephone call or a message of sympathy and comfort can be a blessing. People are blessed by the words we speak. When they see how we come through the sufferings and problems of life with a good attitude and increased faith, in a worthy manner, they too will be blessed.

We have so many precious promises throughout the scriptures. The Lord has promised to be a refuge for the poor and needy, a shelter in the storms of life, a shade from the heat, and warmth from the cold; He has swallowed up death forever, and our sovereign Lord will wipe away the tears from our eyes. He has also said that He will keep in perfect peace him whose mind is steadfast, because he trusts in the Lord. So beloved, do not throw away your confidence, for it will be richly rewarded.

Joshua and Caleb are prime examples of having a healthy attitude toward the "sunset years". God spoke to Joshua and said, "You are old and stricken in years, and there remains yet very much land to be possessed." These men could see beyond the obstacles to taking the land, for they had the faith to believe.

Let us pray that we will have the courage to face the obstacles that confront us, and that we shall bear much fruit for His glory as we wait for His return.

CHAPTER 26

THE STORMS OF LIFE

We have had so many blessings in this great country; so much prosperity, many comforts, and conveniences that we think it's impossible to get along without them. We become ruffled when the power goes off for an hour, and it's a real hardship when the central air is broken for a day. It seems that our lives have to be smoothed out and made easy in every way, and we work very hard to keep it that way. When we begin to take these comforts for granted along comes a hurricane, or an earthquake, floods, tornados, or a great ice storm, and we realize suddenly how fast these natural disasters can cause the loss of all these things.

Do you become fearful and panic when the storms come? That's just what the disciples did when Jesus sent them across the Sea of Galilee. This is a perfect illustration of how we can be in the center of God's will and yet run into terrible problems. Jesus told the disciples to get into the boat and go to the other side of the lake. They were really disturbed when they ran into a storm that brought high winds and heavy waves. They panicked and cried out in fear and in that moment of crisis they forgot that Jesus had told them to go to the other side — He didn't say, "Go and sink". His plan was for them to reach the other side of the lake. Jesus came and met the opposition for them, and that is just what He wants to do for you and me. We forget that He promises to be with us and to meet our every need.

What happens when the storms of life hit at us on every corner? So often I'm afraid it is, "Lord, where are you anyway?" It's so easy to become fearful and lose hope. We become discouraged and feel that we aren't good enough or great enough to be helped. So many of the saints will say, "What have I done to deserve this tragic situation?" Beloved, be assured of one thing, for even the most insignificant saint has His undivided attention. He even knows the number of hairs on your head. The many sufferings, trials, tribulations, losses or whatever heartache you may be experiencing now, God has permitted it for a purpose. We may never know or understand in this lifetime, but we do know that He remains our sovereign God, and He does keep His promises, and can bring deliverance and victory regardless of the circumstances.

Nothing can touch the child of God without His permission. Do we really believe this? We see in Job's life how Satan had to go to God to get permission before he could do anything to Job or his possessions. After losing all his children and possessions, we are told that Job did not sin by charging God with wrongdoing. He fell to the ground in worship to the Lord. He said, "But He knows the way that I take; when He has tested me, I will come forth as gold" (Job 23:10). And the Lord blessed the latter part of Job's life more than the first.

I believe that God knows just how far He can go with each of His children. He also knows just how much we want His will in our life. The Lord wants to reveal Himself in suffering through the believer, and we forget that suffering is allowed by God even if He lets the enemy bring it. He has promised not to put upon us more than we are able to stand. I'm thankful for this promise! Have you wondered why some of God's children seemingly go through trials all the time? As soon as one is over, there is always another one, and it seems that He allows some of the saints to suffer more than others. I wonder if it is because some can bear more without falling to pieces. When we go through the fires, He is right there with us, just as He went through the den of lions with Daniel. He wants the saints to reflect His image, but if the Lord put some of His children in the fires, there wouldn't be anything left but ashes!

When going through great trials, it really should draw us to the Word. As we seek Him and His promises, we are encouraged and will be able to keep on keeping on. "I am the Lord your God, who teaches you what is best for you, who directs you in the way you should go" (Isa. 48:17). We must keep our eyes on the Lord and reflect on His goodness and grace. It also helps to look back and see how He met certain situations in our life. As we think on His watch care over us, we will become thankful and begin to praise Him. One promise that is very meaningful to me is "The Lord will rescue me from every evil attack and will bring me safely to His heavenly kingdom" (2 Tim. 4:18). He may be working out my inheritance in glory. Here we worry, fret, and fume over our earthly possessions that can be taken from us by robbers and thieves, but over there they are secure forever! We really should be busy laying up our treasures in heaven. The storms of life that come at us are devastating, but here they are called light afflictions that last but for a moment. They never seem light to us, but compared to the glory that shall be revealed alongside of what our Lord suffered for us, they are light.

God sent a storm to His disobedient servant Jonah, and all the people on the boat with him were in danger. This happens many times if we have been living in disobedience. Those people close to us will hurt also. When the storm did not get any better, the men threw Jonah overboard. Then he was really in trouble. The Lord had prepared a great fish to swallow up Jonah, and he had to spend three awful days and nights inside the dark stomach of the fish. Jonah knew that there was no one else that could help him now but God, so he began to cry out to Him. He told the Lord he would obey him now. Then the Lord spoke to the fish and it threw up Jonah on to dry land. After that he did go to Nineveh and preach as God had commanded him to do when he started out. That was a terrible experience. It certainly would have been better had he gone to Nineveh in the beginning. So many times we too can bring storms upon us because of disobedience. It is so much better to be like Daniel and purpose in your heart to obey God and live for Him each day.

We are not used to suffering from storms and being deprived of our modern conveniences. We covet the things of this life when we should be seeking and living for eternity! We are so taken up with the present it is even difficult to pray unselfishly. Beloved, even if what you are going through now as loving discipline, remember it is a sure sign that God loves you. He wants you to have the assurance that as you trust Him that your steps are being ordered in the way that you should go. He wants you to have the rock-solid peace and security that all Christians have available to them in Jesus Christ, which can carry them through any storm.

Dear friend, is it raining hard on you tonight? It is indeed raining on many of God's children, and the storm may be growing stronger, but our great Shepherd sees the sweet flower of faith which is springing up in your life under those very trials. You may shrink from the suffering, but God sees the tender compassion for other sufferers which is finding birth in your soul. So let us keep our eyes on Him who promises to bring deliverance and not on the stormy winds that blow against us! He has never promised an easy passage, only a safe landing.

CHAPTER 27

PHILIPPIANS 4:19

When you read Philippians 4:19, "And my God will meet all your needs according to His glorious riches in Christ Jesus," can you really believe this promise? You might say you believe it is true, but do you really believe God means what He said is for you? It seems that we have lost the sense of the reality of God. He is real and supplies your needs just as he did for Abraham, Moses and Elijah.

He fulfilled this great promise to Ollie Hough. For over sixty years He met her every need. She was totally dependent upon her Lord. He never once let her down. She always took her needs to the Lord in prayer and regardless of how impossible they seemed, He was there to help. There is no limit to what God is able to do! He wants us to claim these wonderful riches that He has for us. Pour out your deepest desires to the Lord in prayer.

You may be in deep trouble and feel that God has forsaken you, but dear saint our feelings have nothing to do with the fact that our Lord is still with us and He will keep His word! In the last verse of Matthew, Jesus said, "I am with you always." Many times in scripture He said that He will never leave you or forsake you. Are you suffering from loneliness? Many people are in despair over this affliction. Jesus can be your friend who will stick closer than a brother. Then reach out to the family of God for there are

CHAPTER 28

KNOWING GOD

I n the Old Testament God took a people unto Himself because He wanted to be their God. He wanted to fellowship with them, and He longed for a close, intimate relationship so that He could direct their paths and their ways. He longed to show His great power and glory among them. Over and over again He revealed and manifested Himself to the people. He showed them great miracles, signs and wonders, opened up the Red Sea and took them across on dry ground, and brought water out of a rock and food out of heaven. They were covered with a cloud by day and fire by night. He brought down kings and kingdoms. Angels came and ministered, and even after all the miracles and countless blessings; they still didn't really know God. The Scriptures tell us that they turned back, tempted God and limited the Holy One of Israel.

Beloved, this same God is with us today, and He is still looking for people that will allow Him to be God. We have His Word, but do we take time to really know the truth of the Word? Could it be that we have allowed the cares of this world to keep us from really seeking Him? When we become so busy and distracted by life's problems, it seems that we neglect the most important things. What can we do? Jesus said, "Search the Scriptures" and that takes time. He has given us promises for every area of our lives. He has told us that He is the same God today as He was in ages past. Paul tells us in Romans that

> For I am convinced that neither death nor life, neither angels nor demons, neither the present nor the future, nor any powers, neither height nor depth, nor anything else in all creation, will be able to separate us from the love of God that is in Christ Jesus our Lord. (Rom. 8:38–39)

It is hard for us to comprehend such love, but He tells us to "Call unto me ... and I will show you great and mighty things" Jer. 33:3). God's love has no ending, and His grace cannot be measured. He is always there waiting for us to turn to Him. The world may turn against you and your closest friends may betray you, but God tells you to come to him for he is your refuge and strength; and he will never leave you or forsake you." How encouraging and comforting is His Word!

This old world is so wicked today, and the saints are being burdened with heartaches of every kind. There is so much loneliness! Remember the lonely Samaritan woman at the well? When she came to draw water, Jesus talked to her, and she was shocked. She had faced much rejection and expected no one would speak to her, but He forgave her, transformed her life and made her a new person. She went out to share with joy the miracle that had happened to her that day. Jesus didn't condone what she had done nor did He condemn, but He set her free to become the person she was created to be. There are things in our lives that put us under bondage, and it may not be immorality as the Samaritan woman but we also need to be set free. Whatever we think about the most becomes an idol in our heart. Ask the Lord to show you what it is that needs to go, and then lay it on the altar. Let Him bear your burdens, help you solve your problems, direct and lead you. We need that joy, hope and peace that only the Lord gives. As we sit at the feet of Jesus and learn of Him, all of these blessings will fall upon us. The world can never satisfy or offer us that sweet fellowship, nor can it give us hope and encouragement for the future after life has dealt its many blows.

Fear and anxiety it will keep us from trusting Him. Often when we trials come upon us, I'm afraid we call everyone else before we remember to call unto the one who is able to help. In Isaiah 43 we read, "When you pass through the waters, I will be with you, and when you pass through the rivers, they will not sweep over you ... for I am the Lord, your God ... you are precious and honored in my sight ... do not be afraid for I am with you" (Isa. 43:2–5). He goes on to say, "I will accomplish all that I please" (Isa. 44:28), and "I am the Lord and there is no other" (Isa 45:5).

Sometimes it is difficult to find the time to be alone with the Lord, and especially when you have a heavy work load. Then of our enemy will do everything in his power to interfere, but dear friend, there is always a way. Susanna Wesley was a mother of nineteen children, and the most famous of them were John and Charles. She always managed to get alone with the Lord. It is written that she would throw her apron over her head. When the children saw that they would know she was to be left alone.

The Psalmist said, "Be still, and know that I am God" (Ps. 46:10). It may even take a sick bed for some of us to get to know Him better. As we study the life of David. He could testify to the fact that God was faithful and trustworthy through all his many trials. In one place he said that it was good that he had been afflicted for he had gotten to know God better. He valued God's Word so much that he said, "It is more precious to me than thousands of pieces of silver and gold" (Ps. 119:72).

The Word became flesh and dwelt among us that He might make us know the mind of God, the love, mercy, purpose and the will of God. As we get to know these things, we get to really know the heart of God. Do you know Him as Redeemer? It took His precious blood to pay the penalty for our sins. He laid down His life on a cross to shed His blood in order to redeem us. He was the lamb without blemish and without spot! Do you recall that when

Jesus was placed inside the tomb, not only did they roll a stone over the opening, but they sealed it, and placed a Roman soldier to guard the place? Do you know what happened? The combined forces of hell could not succeed in keeping Him there. That very same Jesus who arose in spite of soldiers and a sealed stone is coming again soon, and we will spend eternity with Him.

I am positively certain that coming to know the Lord as He really is will bring comfort, joy, and peace to troubled hearts. If you know Him, you will love Him, for to know Him is to love Him.

Jacob could not understand why his dear son had to be taken from him. He had to wait for many years before he was to know that God had allowed him to go before them into Egypt to preserve the nation during the famine years. Joseph had to wait in the prison until God was ready to use him as a great leader. Perhaps in your life you have had to wait when running or marching would have been much easier.

Job was able to come to that place of rest as he waited on the Lord, for he knew that God had everything under His control regardless of the terrible circumstances. It must have seemed like a long waiting period, but he declared that God would see him through it all. He began to see that he was being tested for a purpose. Some of the lessons in life cannot be learned just by studying the scriptures. They are learned through experience, and Job had plenty of that. We need to rest in the loving hand of God for He knows what is best for each one of His children.

When we insist on helping God fight our battles, it hinders His working, and it is not that He won't help us, but He can't while we are in the way. It may be that the waiting is to renew our strength for a greater victory in the future. We cannot rush God for He is never in a hurry. Don't give in to despair, for the Lord will stretch forth His hand against the wrath of our enemies and perfect that which concerns us, and He will make the attack to fail.

Perhaps you have waited and prayed for many long years, and still there is no answer. Are you at the breaking point and ready to give it all up as hopeless? Go back to the special promises He has given you and then move on in faith.

> Be still before the Lord and wait patiently for Him;
> do not fret when men succeed in their ways, when
> they carry out their wicked schemes ... for the power
> of the wicked will be broken ... For the Lord loves
> the just and will not forsake His faithful ones ... wait
> for the Lord and keep His way (Ps. 37:7,17,28,34)

The Lord will answer your heart cry, according to the multitude of His tender mercies. His timing is perfect! When that timing is right He will do exceeding abundantly above all that you could ever ask or even think.

There is a wonderful promise in Isaiah 30:18, "Yet the Lord longs to be gracious to you; He rises to show you compassion. For the Lord is a God of justice. Blessed are all who wait for Him!" When you and I get in step with Him, life will be much easier for us. We need to come to the point of trust where we can say, "I have a loving heavenly Father who wants the very best for me, and I am willing to wait on Him no matter how long it may take!"

CHAPTER 30

KEEP ON PRAYING

Jesus told his disciples the parable of the persistent widow in Luke 18:1–8 and in the first verse of that chapter he speaks to us as well as the disciples. He said that "they should always pray and not give up" (Luke 18:1). I believe He is reminding us that we should not be discouraged and stop, but to keep on praying even when things continue as they are. It is very difficult to imagine what life would be like if Jesus had given up His life of obedience before His Heavenly Father. Pray continually, Paul tells us. There is no relationship in our lives that is more important than our relationship with our great God, and we must not allow anything to hinder that constant, faithful commitment to prayer.

At times of crisis, even the most hardened agnostics and atheists can become instant believers. Hopefully, most of the time, our lives are not marked by periods of desperate circumstances. We do, however, face difficulties and problems each day and often these occurrences can cause us to become discouraged, and we lose hope. The Lord knows our weaknesses and realizes there are many forces working against us to keep us from coming to Him who is able to give us the encouragement we need. He says, "Call to me, and I will answer you, and show you great and mighty things, which you do not know" (Jer. 33:3 NKJV). Our Sovereign Lord says that "Is anything too hard for me" (Jer. 32:27). So beloved, when we feel the doom and gloom overtaking us, it is time to confess our total helplessness and to call out as Jehoshaphat did with his people, "For we have no power to face this vast army that is attacking us. We do not know what to do, but our eyes are upon you" (2 Chron.20:12). God always comes through, just as he did for his people there. These people were alarmed, but they were not immobilized. They took action to face their problems, and God was there to help them and to defeat the enemy. The same God is in our midst today. He is always within reach, and never too busy to hear us when we call.

The Lord can manifest his power today just as he did when he was with Moses, Elijah or Jehoshaphat. We need a spirit of expectation. Are we expecting God to come down and undertake for us as he did for Israel? God will see to it that every force that is working against you will be destroyed. He has promised not to withhold any good thing from His children. Then why do we begin to doubt the word of God? I believe we begin to look at the situation rather than at the word of God for He has told us that nothing is too difficult for him. He is the same, yesterday, today and forever. In the 10th chapter of Mark, Jesus was talking to his disciples and said to them, "With man this is impossible, but not with God, all things are possible with God" (Mark 10:27).

It is easy to trust in God when things are going well, when food is on the table, gas in the car, and money in the bank; however, where do we go when our world begins to unravel? Will we remain faithful then? What will we do when wickedness is on the march at full gallop and the enemy comes in like a flood? What happens when God seems to be silent as we pray? Will we be able to trust Him then? James tells us to consider it pure joy whenever you face trials for the testing of faith develops perseverance. Perseverance must finish its work so that you may be mature and complete, not lacking anything. He goes on to say that if we need wisdom we should ask God, who gives generously to all. When we ask, we must believe and not doubt, because he who doubts is like a wave of the sea, blown prayerlessness prevails. We need to be awakened to a sense of need and utter dependence upon God. Jesus said, "Apart from me you can do nothing" (John 15:5). Humble yourselves in the sight of the Lord, and He shall lift you up. The first condition is that we should be humble.

The second condition which is to pray cannot be met until we first humble ourselves. Proud men can say prayers, but prayer is more than words; it is an expression of a sincere desire toward God. It is the heart that is humbled by the power of the Holy Spirit that really prays. God still says,

> If my people, who are called by my name, will humble themselves and pray and seek my face and turn from their wicked ways, then will I hear from heaven and will forgive their sin and will heal their land. (2 Chron. 7:14–15)

Now we come to the third condition which is perhaps the most crucial step of all toward revival. Seek His face. Isaiah realized that the face of God was turned away from Israel, for he said,

> Surely the arm of the Lord is not too short to save, not His ear too dull to hear. But your iniquities have separated you from your God; your sins have hidden His face from you, so that He will not hear. (Isa.59:1–2)

They were powerless because they were not in fellowship with God. They had their form of religion and went through all the ceremonies, but God said of them, "These people come near to me with their mouth and honor me with their lips, but their hearts are far from me" (Isa. 29:13). Beloved, are you enjoying fellowship with the Lord, and are you conscious of His presence? To many people today, the Lord is not a reality. Having a sense of His abiding presence makes us guard against those things that are not pleasing to Him. God help us to seek a more intimate relationship with Him. When we seek His face we will automatically meet the fourth condition, to turn from our wicked ways! God has a great deal to say about repentance for His children. In Revelation He says, "Those whom I love I rebuke and discipline so be earnest and repent" (Rev.3:19). Repent or perish, we are told, and this is a stern warning to the church today. God is true to His Word just as He was in Noah's day. We know that destruction was brought on Sodom and Gomorrah, and God allowed Judah to go into captivity for seventy years because of their disobedience. How can we expect our country that was founded on Christian principles, to escape judgment when we have gone so far away from God? In Galatians we read,

> Do not be deceived: God cannot be mocked. A man reaps what he sows. The one who sows to please his sinful nature, from that nature will reap destruction; the one who sows to please the Spirit, from the Spirit will reap eternal life. (Galatians 6:7)

This can also be applied to a nation.

We hear a lot today about the love and mercy of God, and it is true, but there is a truth about the fear of the Lord which we don't hear very often. God hates sin though he loves the sinner, and He has given us instructions all through the Scriptures. It is through the fear of the Lord that a man avoids evil, and the fear of the Lord will teach a man wisdom. We are drawn away from God just as Israel was by the pleasures of this life. James tells us, "You adulterous people, don't you know that friendship with the world is hatred toward God? Anyone who chooses to be a friend of the world becomes an enemy of God. Who is wise and understanding among you? Let him show it by his good lite, by deeds done in the humility that comes from wisdom" (James 4:4). We put our trust into so many worthless things, and though some may be considered good, God wants to be first in our life. In Lamentations 3:31 we read, "For men are not cast off by the Lord forever. Though he brings grief, he will show compassion, so great is his unfailing love. For he does not willingly bring affliction or grief to the children of men" (Lam. 3:33–35). Great is His faithfulness to us!

We can't work up a revival, and there is no way we can bring in special speakers to make it happen in a few days' time. It happens because God's people call out to Him. Why did God base the conditions of His promises on prayer? Prayer proves that we believe God, and we know and expect something to happen when we pray! There is power in united prayer, so let us join forces with those who have dedicated themselves to call upon the Lord for a mighty awakening for the church. What a great and blessed work, and what an assurance we have of an abundant answer. Christians everywhere must get to their knees to pray for revival. Joel says,

> Blow the trumpet in Zion, sound the alarm on my holy hill. Let all who live in the land tremble, for the day of the Lord is coming. It is close at hand. Even now, declares the Lord, return to me with all your heart. (Joel 2:1, 12)

May God give us such an intense, unselfish love for Him and for His people that faith will be impelled to hold on until He answers our heart cry!

CHAPTER 32

THE DAY OF HIS COMING

The Bible is a message to all mankind and a promise of hope and encouragement to those who place their trust in the Lord Jesus Christ. Some of the signs of the times are very troubling to us, and especially when we do not know the scriptures. The Lord has given us the prophecy scriptures that we might have the assurance that He is in control. All of the events must happen to bring about His purposes. They are signs to show us that we are getting close to the Lord's return, first to catch away all His followers and later to rescue Israel and reign from Jerusalem for a thousand years.

This world is not our home, but so many Christians have put down roots so deep that they have forgotten that Jesus said to do His work until He comes. We all must go about our daily lives, but our hearts should be crying, "Even so, come Lord Jesus" (Rev. 22:20 NKJV). There is a verse in Titus that says, "Looking for that blessed hope, and the glorious appearing of the great God and our Savior Jesus Christ" (Titus 2:13 NKJV). "Now there is in store for me the crown of righteousness, which the Lord, the righteous judge, will award to me on that day — and not only to me, but also to all who have longed for his appearing" (2 Timothy 4:8). Our great God will reward us who believe and look for His return! Do you yearn for the day when He will appear? Are you looking forward to that day, or does it cause your heart to fear?

When we look forward to that blessed hope of Christ's return, it is not a form of escapism as so many have said, but one of the things we were meant to do. When we live in expectation of His soon return, it will promote an unselfish lifestyle, a pure heart, and a life of active service. The Lord is going to come again, so we need to be ready! There are over three hundred references in the New Testament about Christ's return. We know we aren't to just stand looking up for Him, nor do we have to talk about it all the time. He did say to be alert and aware that He would soon return. We must get on with our business of living a holy life and giving out the good news.

Know this first of all, that in the last days mockers will come with their mocking, following after their own lusts, and saying, "Where is the promise of His coming? For ever since the fathers fell asleep, all continues just as it was from the beginning of creation" (2 Peter 3–4). This is so true! We will hear many skeptics say these things. Well, they are just fulfilling prophecy. Jesus said,

> Therefore keep watch, because you do not know on what day your Lord will come. But understand this: If the owner of the house had known at what time of night the thief was coming, he would have kept watch and would not have let his house be broken into. So you also must be ready, because the Son of Man will come at an hour when you do not expect him. (Matt. 24:42–44)

The midnight hour is surely upon us and we listen, "Behold He comes!" We hear so much today about the soon return of the Lord, and the signs which He gave us are literally being fulfilled. He said,

> You will hear of wars and rumors of wars ... Nation
> will rise against nation ... There will be famines and
> earthquakes ... (many) will betray and hate each
> other ... Because of the increase of wickedness, the
> love of most will grow cold. (Matt. 24:6–13)

Daily the news shows us these things are happening all around the
world. Our cities and even the small towns are covered in wickedness!
There is no safety except to those who call on the Lord. As God
promised Israel plenty and safety when they obeyed his commands,
blessings and safety are ours when we seek him.

Clearly, we are running out of time. The cup of man's iniquity
is almost full. Our Lord's return is growing near. Someone has
said, "Watch Israel if you want to know where we are on God's
prophetic calendar". The Book of Revelation is not just a book of
ancient history. It's actually a prophetic panorama of God's sovereign
plan of the ages. God wants us to be equipped with knowledge and
discernment necessary to be able to recognize the signs of the times,
and Israel is God's timepiece. Soon the trumpet will sound. What
a time that will be! Those who are truly watching and waiting are
filled with joy and rapture such as nothing else can give.

Dear saints, may we all watch, wait, work and pray for the soon
coming of the Lord, for

> We will not all sleep, but we will all be changed
> — in a flash, in the twinkling of an eye, at the
> last trumpet.... Therefore, my dear brothers, stand
> firm. Let nothing move you. Always give yourselves
> fully to the work of the Lord, because you know
> that your labor in the Lord is not in vain. (1 Cor.
> 15:51–52, 58)

CHAPTER 33

REJOICE!

When the apostle Paul wrote the book of Philippians he was under the control of a Roman soldier and in chains. Can you imagine that he could still say to rejoice? He not only says that we Christians should rejoice, but that we should learn to be content. Paul says,

> I have learned to be content whatever the circumstances. I know what it is to be in need, and I know what it is to have plenty. I have learned the secret of being content in any and every situation, whether well fed or hungry, whether living in plenty or in want. (Phil 4:11–12)

He had suffered greatly in three shipwrecks, and exposed to death again and again, was beaten many times with rods, stoned, insulted, and persecuted by the Jews and Gentiles. He knew hunger and thirst, and there was a weakness that he called a thorn in the flesh. Yet, he could still say that he had learned to give thanks, to rejoice and to be content! Amazing Paul! No, amazing Lord who was giving him strength, courage and wisdom as he lived his life through him.

Paul was totally submitted to the Lord. He was able to say, "I count it all joy!" The mind of Christ in the believer will bring joy and will give glory to God.

> Rejoice in the Lord always. I will say it again: Rejoice! Let your gentleness be evident to all. The Lord is near. Do not be anxious about anything, but in everything, by prayer and petition, with thanksgiving, present your requests to God. (Phil. 4:5–6)

He not only tells us once to rejoice but repeats the command. Now how are we to rejoice when we are going through dark and difficult circumstances? It is easy to rejoice when we're on a mountain-top, but what do you do when you're in the valley? Life is full of valley experiences and we must learn to deal with them. It is so tempting to start complaining, but as we study this epistle you can see that joy is the theme. So even in the midst of suffering, Paul had learned to rejoice. It was a choice he made for he knew that God would balance things out in eternity. He had learned to celebrate life and to anoint others with the oil of gladness. One who does not experience the joy of the Lord has no power with man or with God. When we are filled with thanksgiving and gladness, it will become contagious. May it be a constant overflowing of the abundant life. He wants us to trust Him so fully that we worry about nothing, and pray about everything, no matter how large or small. When we leave our burdens at the feet of Jesus, He promises to give us that wonderful peace that passes all understanding.

Beloved, when we come to the place of total dependence on God alone, we then will find that blessed rest for our soul. Regardless of what is going on around us, we will find that inward peace that is so priceless. Quite often God will allow us to lose our joy in everything else until we completely find our joy in Him alone. Then He will restore our joy threefold. Life will truly take on a new meaning! Every day will be meaningful. "This is the day the Lord has made, let us rejoice and be glad in it!" (Ps. 118:24). In Proverbs we read that a relaxed attitude lengthens a man's life: "A heart at peace gives life to the body" (Prov. 14:30). Your life can be filled with laughter. "A cheerful heart is good medicine, but a crushed spirit dries up the bones" (Prov. 17:22). Sooner or later we will all meet with adversity, but even in the dark times we must be able to look on the bright side and know that we are looking toward eternity. God may be using these very things to draw us closer to Him.

David must have felt that he was secure on his mountaintop and that he would be exempt from problems that ordinary folk experience, for when an illness hit him it brought great sorrow and devastation. He knew he had enemies that would gloat over his condition. Have you ever felt that way? Do you ever feel that God has turned His face from you? Our minds go berserk wondering if this or that should happen or that. Even when we think we are doing what God wants, it seems as though he is not there. See how David expresses these same thoughts in Psalm 30, but also see how he rejoices and praises God for his's faithfulness.

> O Lord my God, I called to you for help and you healed me. O Lord, you brought me up from the grave; you spared me from going down into the pit. Sing to the Lord, you saints of His; praise His holy name. For His anger lasts only a moment, but His favor lasts a lifetime; weeping may remain for a night, but rejoicing comes in the morning. When I felt secure, I said, I will never be shaken. O Lord, when you favored me, you made my mountain stand firm; but when you hid your face, I was dismayed. To you, O Lord, I called; to the Lord I cried for mercy; ... You turned my wailing into dancing; you removed my sackcloth and clothed me with joy, that my heart may sing to you and not be silent. O Lord my God, I will give you thanks forever. (Psalm 30:2–12)

It is difficult to face the challenges of life with optimism and the joy of the Lord. It certainly cannot come from what we see all about us, but it must come because we know that our Lord is sovereign and He will triumph in the end. Our joy is not of this world but comes through knowing our Lord Jesus Christ. He has told us that we have an inheritance, incorruptible, undefiled, that fades not away, reserved in heaven and ready to be revealed in the last days.

The Lord told His disciples that hard times were coming for them, and that the hard times meant blessing. This is what He said,

> Blessed are you when men hate you, when they exclude you and insult you and reject your name as evil, because of the Son of Man. Rejoice in that day and leap for joy, because great is your reward in heaven. For that is how their fathers treated the prophets. (Luke 6:22–23).

He said they were to look upon these experiences with thanksgiving and exultation for the rewards will be great in heaven. Joy runs through the Scriptures like a song. Beloved, let us refuse to be troubled by the trouble all around us for the Prince of Peace is at hand. Refuse to put your trust in any but God Himself. We have so much to rejoice in. The Lord will dwell with us in the New Jerusalem, and He will wipe every tear from our eyes. There will be no more death or mourning, crying or pain, for the old order of things has passed away. Now that is enough to bring encouragement and hope to the heaviest heart. Rejoice always!

Whatever your difficulty may be right now, remember "Weeping may remain for a night, but joy comes in the morning" (Ps, 30:5). Cling to this promise for it was made by a loving God.

CHAPTER 34

WAKE UP AMERICA

We are held in the grip of such a spirit of apathy in the nation that even the perilous conditions that are prevailing all over the world do not stir our consciousness enough to draw us away from our selfish pursuits and interests. Beloved, we need to be called to a real dedicated prayer effort against the forces of evil! The church can do nothing greater than this. We see in 1 Timothy 2:1–2 that God wants us to pray for our leaders; "I urge them, first of all, that requests, prayers, intercession and thanksgiving be made for everyone ... for kings and all those in authority, that we may live peaceful and quiet lives in all godliness and holiness." If our freedoms are taken away, we will not be able to worship as we have in the past. By praying for them like this, the church helps those in authority to exercise their powers wisely and justly. When rulers rule properly, their subjects can live quiet and peaceable lives, the opposite of which is unrest and turmoil, which describes this present evil world about us.

We also need to pray for our spiritual leaders. Better praying in the pew will make better preaching in the pulpit. What kind of church do you attend? Is it alive where you are fed spiritually? Are you being discipled? Maybe your church is dead, compromising and not at all provoking to righteousness. Our churches should be feeding us the pure word of God and we should be growing in holiness.

When we consider the prayerlessness and indifference and self-centered way of life today, how pointed is the admonition in the following scriptures:

The hour has come for you to wake up from your slumber, ... The night is nearly over; the day is almost here. So let us put aside the deeds of darkness ... and do not think about how to gratify the desires of the sinful nature. (Rom. 13:11–12)

We need to be awakened to a sense of responsibility that will cause us to seek an outpouring of the Holy Spirit. God is always with us and promises to never leave us nor forsake us. If there ever was a time when a united prayer effort was needed, it is now!

Jeremiah prophesied that all shepherds (or pastors) who refuse to seek God in prayer will fail: "The shepherds are senseless and do not inquire of the Lord; so they do not prosper and all their flock is scattered" (Jer. 10:21). In the church today we are seeing leaders that become lazy and neglectful in feeding the flock the spiritual food that they need. They turn to books and commentaries for their sermons instead of seeking to give them God's Word that is fresh from Him. As a result, there is no power to feed the sheep, and as a consequence, the sheep are being scattered!

It would be easy to look around and feel nothing but despair. The Bible declares in Leviticus 18 that when a society gives itself over to gross immorality, the very land it inhabits will vomit out its people. We have seen how television with its violence, crime, and low moral standards has changed our nation. God has been ruled out of our schools, and children no longer are being taught right from wrong. Standards are no longer taught. There are so many broken homes and emotionally damaged people. America needs the greatest outpouring of the Holy Spirit in the history of the world because sin is rampant today. We're living in such a violent society that the streets are dangerous even in daylight. Every Christian should use whatever time he has to pray as Abraham prayed for Sodom. We should speak out as the prophet Jonah did when he warned Nineveh of the coming doom. We are to call the nation to repentance as Jeremiah did,

> Tell them everything I command you; do not omit a word. Perhaps they will listen and each will turn from his evil way. Then I will relent and not bring on them the disaster I was planning because of the evil they have done" (Jer. 26:2–3)

The priests, the prophets and all the people seized him and threatened to kill him. Ezekiel warned the people of Israel over and over again that God was calling them to repent, but they would not hear. We should speak out with courage and boldness as Paul called to the Jews and the Gentiles.

There is power to be found as we seek God, and victory to live each day as He would have us live! The eyes of the Lord are upon the righteous, and His ears are open unto their cry. Even though we are seeing an acceleration of wickedness that is far more amazing and frightful than the changes that we have seen in the past, God yearns to show us His power and strength in our day. Let us not be like Israel and close our ears to His voice calling us to wake up for the time is short!

God asks all of His servants to continually step out in obedience to Him and remain faithful. If you will stay true to the Lord and not try to measure yourself by anything except your own love for Jesus, then you can be assured He will be there to bless you as you speak out for Him. Determine in your heart to put His interests first and to seek Him. Beloved give God no rest! Keep coming to Him in faith until He pours out a mighty measure of the Holy Spirit. This is the only hope we have for America and the church. God is all we need! "Blessed is the nation whose God is the Lord". (Ps 33:12).

Printed in the United States
By Bookmasters